A

A

le ... ... freelance journalist for a
variety of publications and was a columnist for the *Nottingham
Evening Post*.

Her stage plays include *Be My Baby* (Soho Theatre), *Satin
'n' Steel* (Nottingham Playhouse/Bolton Octagon); *Ladies'
Day* (Hull Truck), *Bollywood Jane* (Leicester Haymarket),
The Wills's Girls (Tobacco Factory Bristol/BBC Radio Four),
Players Angels, *Last Stop Louisa's* and *The Boy on the Hill*
(New Perspectives). She has also written three youth theatre
plays and a stage adaptation of *Saturday Night and Sunday
Morning*.

For more information visit www.amandawhittington.com

Amanda Whittington

LADIES' DAY

NICK HERN BOOKS

London

www.nickhernbooks.co.uk

A Nick Hern Book

Ladies' Day first published in Great Britain as a paperback original in 2006 by Nick Hern Books Limited, 14 Larden Road, London W3 7ST

Ladies' Day copyright © 2006 Amanda Whittington

Amanda Whittington has asserted his right to be identified as the author of this work

Cover image by Hull Truck; design by Ned Hoste/2H

Typeset by Country Setting, Kingsdown, Kent CT14 8ES
Printed and bound in Great Britain by Biddles, King's Lynn

A CIP catalogue record for this book is available from the British Library

ISBN-13   978 1 85459 950 6
ISBN-10   1 85459 950 X

Ladies' Day was first presented by Hull Truck Theatre Company at Hull Truck Theatre on 2 June 2005 with the following cast:

PEARL	Annie Sawle
JAN	Sue McCormick
SHELLEY	Jemma Walker
LINDA	Lucy Beaumont
JOE/ FRED/JIM/ PATRICK/KEVIN/ BARRY	Martin Barrass

Director   Gareth Tudor Price
Designer   Richard Foxton

Characters

PEARL, *a fish packer, mid-fifties*

JAN, *a fish packer, mid-forties*

SHELLEY, *a fish packer, mid-twenties*

LINDA, *a fish packer, mid-twenties*

JOE, *their supervisor*

FRED, *a ticket tout*

JIM McCORMACK, *a TV pundit*

PATRICK, *an Irish jockey*

KEVIN, *a gambler*

BARRY, *a bookie*

All male parts can be played by one actor.

The play is set in Hull and York, June 2005.

ACT ONE

Scene One

Fish plant, Hull. June 2005. Morning. PEARL, JAN, SHELLEY *and* LINDA *are hard at work.*

Their job is to weigh, trim and pack individual fillets of fish. The fillets are delivered to them on trays from the smoking-ovens. PEARL *and* SHELLEY *take a fillet from the tray, trim it and put it in a box.* JAN *weighs and seals the boxes.* LINDA *assembles the boxes.*

Their movements are quick and dexterous. They wear no jewellery or make-up; just a hairnet, overall and Wellington boots, all white, with body-warmers beneath. The plant is cold and damp; the routine is relentless.

JAN. What d'you have for your tea last night?

LINDA. Pizza.

SHELLEY. Slimfast.

PEARL. Mick took me down the road, it's two for one on a Tuesday.

JAN. We had pork chops, baby new potatoes, frozen carrots, fresh broccoli and Bisto gravy. Pork chops are on offer at Iceland.

PEARL. We had Cajun chicken.

JAN. Was it spicy?

PEARL. Sorta.

JAN. I can't be doing with all that.

LINDA. I heard that song on the radio this morning, what's it called?

SHELLEY. Can you be a bit more specific?

LINDA. It's by him. Michael Jackson.

SHELLEY. 'Thriller'?

LINDA. The one about the boy?

JAN. 'Ben'.

LINDA. That's it.

PEARL. Ben's about a rat.

SHELLEY. A what?.

> LINDA *sings the first line of 'Ben' by Michael Jackson.*
> JAN *joins in.*

> Can't you sing summat cheerful?

> LINDA *sings the first line of 'Is This the Way to Amarillo'*
> *by Tony Christie.*

> Friggin' hell.

> JAN *and* PEARL *join in.*

> Why can't you like what's boss, Linda?

JAN. Boss?

LINDA. He is boss.

PEARL. You're back in vogue, aren't you, Lin?

LINDA. Yeh.

PEARL. Who'd have thought it, ey? Your favourite singer topping the charts.

LINDA. And doing concerts.

JAN. He put on a good show, I'll give him that.

LINDA. He were brilliant.

SHELLEY. He were bloody awful.

PEARL. You were singing along to Amarillo, I saw yer.

LINDA. I saw yer.

SHELLEY. You're only twenty-four, for God's sake. Why can't you like Blue?

LINDA. Who?

SHELLEY *sings the chorus of 'All Rise' by Blue.*

JAN. Claire likes Blue. She's gorra poster.

LINDA. I've gorra Tony Christie poster.

SHELLEY. Oh my God.

JAN. She likes the one with the hair, you know? The one who looks like he's just gorr'up.

SHELLEY. Duncan.

JAN. That's the one.

SHELLEY. He's a nob.

JAN. How do you know?

SHELLEY. 'Cos I've met him, actually.

LINDA. Have yer?

SHELLEY. Yeh, at Waterfront before he were famous. He asked me back to the Holiday Inn but I couldn't be arsed.

PEARL. Shame. You could be gracing the pages of *Hello* by now.

SHELLEY. I've turned down bigger names than him, luv.

PEARL. Like who?

SHELLEY. I'll just say Let Me Entertain You and leave it at that.

PEARL. Oh, Des O'Connor?

SHELLEY. Robbie Williams.

LINDA. Have you met him?

SHELLEY. I bumped into him backstage but he's not my type.

JAN. It's all them tattoos.

PEARL. I think he looks like a chimp.

JAN. I hope our Claire never wants a tattoo.

SHELLEY. Claire? She's not even pierced her ears.

JAN. But you know what students are like.

SHELLEY. Yeh, tossers.

JAN. I've seen 'em with their hair dyed blue an' all sorts.

PEARL. Not Claire.

JAN. How d'you know? She might come home at Christmas with a ring through her nose. It keeps me awake at night, I tell yer.

Enter JOE, *their supervisor.*

JOE. What does?

SHELLEY. The new man in her life.

JAN. Shelley!

JOE. Who's that, then?

SHELLEY. He's a six-foot trawler man, she met him in Rayners.

LINDA. What's his name?

PEARL. It's all right, Lin. She's winding him up.

JOE. Yeh, well, there's overtime going on Sunday.

JAN. I'm in.

LINDA. Me an' all.

SHELLEY. Forget it.

JOE. We've got to get the order out for Tescos.

SHELLEY. I'm busy.

JAN. Doing what?

SHELLEY. Owt but this.

JOE. That's what I like to see. Willing workers. Happy smiling faces. Warms the cockles of my heart.

He laughs.

LINDA. What's so funny?

JOE. Ah, nothing.

LINDA. What?

JOE. Never you mind.

SHELLEY. Gorra secret, have yer?

JOE. No.

SHELLEY. Gorra secret woman?

JOE. I wish. Are you working this overtime or what?

SHELLEY. I'd rather stick pins in my eyes.

JOE. It's double-time.

SHELLEY. Put me down.

JOE. Pearl?

PEARL. Ah, go on, then.

JAN. While you've still got the chance, ey?

SHELLEY. This time next week, you'll be a desperate housewife.

PEARL. A lady of leisure.

JOE. So have you got it then?

PEARL. What?

JOE. Your bus pass.

PEARL. I'm only fifty-five, thanks.

JOE. Early retirement, ey? It's all right for some.

PEARL. I'm not retiring as such, I'm just . . .

SHELLEY. Giving up.

JAN. Winding down.

PEARL. Yeh. Can't wait.

LINDA. Why d'you have to go now though?

PEARL. 'Cos Mick's retired –

SHELLEY. And he's fed up.

PEARL. He wants us to have time for ourselves.

SHELLEY. What? In a caravan at Patrington Haven.

JOE. Trim 'n' pack, girls. Trim 'n' pack; trim 'n' pack.

JAN. There's nowt wrong with Patrington Haven.

SHELLEY. Nowt that a friggin' bomb wouldn't fix. Why couldn't you buy a place in Spain?

PEARL. He had a lump sum not a lottery win.

JAN. Well, I think it's lovely. You've worked hard all these years, you've raised your kids and now you're done. Now it's just you and him.

PEARL. Yeh. Free at last, ey?

JAN. I envy you, Pearl. I look at you and Mick and think, 'That's what a marriage is.' He might not do the hearts and flowers thing but you're together, aren't you? He's there for you and you're there for him. You're rock solid.

PEARL. We're thirty-six years into it, that must count for something.

JAN. So how've you done it? How've you kept it going all these years?

JOE. With batteries.

PEARL. You just do, don't you?

JAN. Come on, tell us the secret.

PEARL. If I knew it, I would. I'd bottle it and make a fortune.

LINDA. We'll miss you, Pearl.

PEARL. Get out. Come Monday, you'll have forgotten all about me.

JOE. Who said that?

LINDA. We'll miss your singing.

SHELLEY. Speak for yourself.

LINDA *sings the chorus of 'Is This the Way to Amarillo'.* PEARL *and* JAN *join in.*

JAN. Our Claire's got her English Literature exam this afternoon.

SHELLEY. I could have gone to college.

JAN. It's not a college, it's a university.

SHELLEY. I had a place. I was going to be a beautician.

PEARL. Why didn't yer?

SHELLEY. I couldn't have done a crack wax.

JAN. You know George Eliot?

LINDA. Him in the warehouse?

JAN. No, *The Mill on the Floss*.

JOE. Is that a pub?

JAN. It's a book by George Eliot, *The Mill on the Floss*. He's a woman, you know?

SHELLEY. Did he have a sex change?

JAN. Of course not, it's the olden days. Her real name's Mary Ann summat.

PEARL. Evans.

JOE. Are you still here?

JAN. Claire says she changed it 'cos women couldn't write books. Then she said, 'When I do mine, it'll be our name on the cover, wait and see.'

LINDA. Tony Christie changed his name.

SHELLEY. Perhaps he's a girl, he bloody sings like one.

LINDA. You said you liked him.

SHELLEY. No, I didn't.

LINDA. Yes, you did. On the bus home from the concert, you said he was brilliant.

SHELLEY. Linda, I was shit-faced.

LINDA. I don't care. You liked him.

JOE. Will you lot get a move-on? We want a thousand boxes out this shift.

SHELLEY. Oh my God!

JAN. What?

SHELLEY. Emmerdale last night.

JAN. Ooh, I know.

SHELLEY. Can you believe her?

JAN. With him?

SHELLEY. He's so gross.

PEARL. She's good though, in't she? That actress, she does it well.

SHELLEY. She's a cow in real life. They're killing her off.

JAN. I can't think of anyone who'd take the part better.

SHELLEY. I can. Me.

PEARL. Me and Mick might take up amateur dramatics.

SHELLEY. Yeh, right.

PEARL. He says we've got to have an 'obby. Summat we can do together.

LINDA. I've never had an 'obby.

SHELLEY. And I never want one, thank you very much.

JAN. Painting, cycling, mountaineering. The world's your oyster.

SHELLEY. Friggin' hell, you'll wish you're back at work.

JAN. So can we finally decide what we're doing?

JOE. Nine-thirty. Tea up.

SHELLEY. For what?

JAN. For Pearl's retirement.

PEARL. I'm not retiring.

JAN. All right, your leaving do. It's high time we sorted summat out.

LINDA. Are we having a party?

PEARL. I don't want a fuss.

JOE. Well, tough. You're not leaving here without a send-off.

SHELLEY. I'll tell you what we should do. Hire one of them great big white limos and go out on the town.

JAN. No chance.

SHELLEY. Everybody looks when you're gerrin' out, they think you're famous.

JOE. They think you're a prat.

JAN. How about a nice meal in a pub?

SHELLEY. How about a punch in the gob?

JAN. All right, what do you suggest that's interesting and special and appropriate?

SHELLEY. Pozition.

JAN. Us?

SHELLEY. There's a VIP bar, there's footballers.

LINDA. They're too old for Pozition.

SHELLEY. Linda, don't be so rude.

PEARL. She's right. We'd look like grab-a-granny night.

SHELLEY. All right, let's all go to yours and knit a cardi.

JOE. Come on, Pearl? I bet you've still got a dream in your pocket.

PEARL. Not really.

JOE. Ah, I bet there's somewhere you'd still like to go, something you'd still like to see.

SHELLEY. Pozition.

LINDA. I don't think she'd like it, Shell.

SHELLEY. We're not all like you, Linda. We don't all stand there dumbstruck when we meet Jason Price.

JAN. Who?

SHELLEY. He only plays for Hull City.

LINDA. I thought he was a bouncer.

JAN. Never mind about him. Pearl?

PEARL. Well, there might have been one thing but it's too late now.

JAN. What?

PEARL. And we couldn't have gone 'cos it's tomorrow.

JOE. What is it?

PEARL. Ladies' Day at Royal Ascot. It's come to York this year.

JAN. I know, I saw it on the telly.

PEARL. I just fancied it, that's all.

JAN. Well, why didn't you say?

PEARL. 'Cos it's a work day and like I said, I don't want a fuss.

SHELLEY. Ladies' Day? Is that them women in the hats?

PEARL. That's it.

SHELLEY. They're rich, them what go there? And some of 'em are famous.

PEARL. Rich, famous, royal.

JAN. We can't go to owt like that, we're not posh.

JOE. You don't have to be.

SHELLEY. Do men go to Ladies' Day an' all?

LINDA. Does Tony Christie?

PEARL. Well, I don't know about him but men in general do.

SHELLEY. So it's like a sorta great big massive party with rich blokes?

PEARL. Yeh.

SHELLEY. All giving it loads?

JOE. I bet you'd get tickets if you turned up.

PEARL. It was sold out months ago.

JOE. I bet you'd get some off the touts.

PEARL. Touts . . . ?

JOE. They'll be there on the gate, I guarantee. Take enough cash and you'll be in.

PEARL. We can't. We'd leave you high and dry.

JOE. I'll get on to the agency, sort summat out.

PEARL. What's come over you all of a sudden?

JOE. Well, Pearl, you're not the only one who's leaving, are yer?

PEARL. What d'you mean?

JOE. Me visa. I got home last night and there's the letter on the mat. Twenty years of saving and dreaming and I've got it. I've bloody gorrit!

PEARL. You're going?!

JOE. Dead right I am.

LINDA. Where?

JOE. Australia, sport. Melbourne, Sydney, Bondi Beach, Ayres Rock.

JAN. When?

JOE. Just as soon as I've got out of this place.

JAN. For how long?

JOE. A whole bloody year.

LINDA. Wow.

SHELLEY. So we've finally got shot of you at last?

PEARL. Come here, you.

PEARL *hugs* JOE.

Well done.

JAN. Yeh. Well done.

JOE. I gave my notice in this morning. I'm packing up my flat.

JAN. That's a bit hasty. I mean, what'll you come back to?

JOE. Who says I am?

SHELLEY. I thought only students went travelling. You'll look more like their dad.

JOE. So? I'd go on a zimmer if I had to.

PEARL. I can't believe you're really going.

JAN. Nor me.

LINDA. It's a long way, in't it?

JOE. It's a world away from this place and I won't be looking back. See you in the canteen.

Exit JOE.

PEARL. Well?

JAN. I can't believe it.

PEARL. Not him. Us. Tomorrow. How about it?

JAN. I can't afford it.

PEARL. Don't you worry about that.

LINDA. Will it be owt like the Tony Christie show?

PEARL. It'll be just like that with horses.

SHELLEY. And rich blokes and champagne.

PEARL. If he can go to Australia, we can go to York.

SHELLEY. Dead right.

PEARL. Royal Ascot, here we come!

Scene Two

Music: 'Is This the Way to Amarillo' by Tony Christie.

The women take off their overalls, hairnets and white wellies to reveal Ascot dresses. They add big hats, bags and shoes, singing along to the song as they go.

Scene Three

York Racecourse. Main Gate. Next day. PEARL, JAN *and* SHELLEY *look around in awe.* JAN *is carrying a large cool bag.*

PEARL. This is it, girls. Royal Ascot.

SHELLEY. Smell that.

JAN. What?

PEARL. Horses?

SHELLEY. Money. Lovely money!

JAN. I've never seen owt like it.

SHELLEY. All the men in whatchercall'em.

PEARL. Monkey suits.

JAN. All the dresses.

SHELLEY. All the hats.

JAN. It's like a great big massive royal wedding.

SHELLEY. Come on, then. Let's get us tickets and get in.

PEARL. We've got to wait for Linda.

SHELLEY. How long does it take to have a pee?

JAN. There's must be a queue.

SHELLEY. You gave her that can of Coke, she'll be hyper.

JAN. She's all right.

SHELLEY. Trust you to bring a packed lunch.

JAN. It's a picnic. That's what you do at Royal Ascot, I saw it on the telly.

SHELLEY. No; that's what you do at Royal Ascot. (*Points.*) You park your Rolls Royce, set your table up behind it and get your butler to serve you champagne. You don't bring cheese and pickle sarnies in a cool bag.

JAN. You'll be glad of 'em later when you see what they're charging.

SHELLEY. I don't care. I've come here to spend, spend, spend.

JAN. You might have. I'm saving every penny –

SHELLEY. For our Claire's education. Yeh, we know.

Beat.

JAN. What did you have for your tea last night?

SHELLEY. Chicken korma.

PEARL. Baked potatoes.

JAN. We had spaghetti bolognese. Claire says that's all they eat at Uni.

SHELLEY. They know how to live.

JAN. How much will they cost, do you think? The tickets. I've brought thirty pounds, I can't stretch no further.

PEARL. It's all right, it's my treat.

JAN. Now hang on a minute –

PEARL. It's my rainy day money.

JAN. You can't spend it on us.

SHELLEY. Yes, she can. Shut up.

PEARL. Let's call it my final fling.

JAN. But what'll your Mick say?

PEARL. He doesn't know I've got it.

JAN. But what if you need it?

PEARL. I won't. What do they look like, do you think?

JAN. Who?

PEARL. Ticket touts.

SHELLEY. Dodgy and shifty, I've seen 'em at shows.

JAN. Is it legal what they do? I mean, I don't want to get into trouble –

SHELLEY. Oh my God!

JAN. What?

SHELLEY. That woman – that hat!

PEARL. There's hundreds of hats.

SHELLEY. That one there, look at it!

They watch an imaginary group of well-dressed women go by.

JAN. Well, I'm sorry, that's just stupid.

SHELLEY. It's designer.

PEARL. It looks more like a wedding cake.

SHELLEY. And yours looks like a bloody currant bun.

PEARL. It's better than that bird-box you're wearing.

JAN. Ladies, please.

SHELLEY. You never said we'd be competing with that.

PEARL. We're not competing with anyone.

SHELLEY. Speak for yourself.

JAN. Does mine look all right?

PEARL. Yeh.

SHELLEY. Yeh.

JAN. I've had it since Kelly's wedding.

SHELLEY. Kelly who?

JAN. She worked on our section, it was way before your time. It was a posh do, that.

PEARL. 'Til the punch-up.

SHELLEY. What happened?

PEARL. The best man hit the groom.

JAN. How long ago was that?

PEARL. Seven years in September.

JAN. Seven years since I last wore a hat.

PEARL. Time flies.

JAN. Don't it just?

Enter FRED, *a ticket tout.*

FRED. Grandstand tickets.

SHELLEY. Girls?

FRED. Anyone for grandstand tickets.

SHELLEY. Over here, mate.

JAN. Keep your voice down.

PEARL. Leave it to me.

FRED. How many, luv?

PEARL. Four.

FRED. Four for the Grandstand. No problem.

FRED *counts out four tickets.*

PEARL. How much?

FRED. You've got a great view of the course from here.
    Restaurants, bars, betting, the lot. You can get to the
    Paddock, see the Royal Enclosure.

PEARL. That's enough of the sales pitch. How much?

FRED. Two grand.

PEARL. How much?

FRED. Two thousand pounds.

PEARL. You're joking?

JAN. Five hundred pounds each?

FRED. Six. I'm doing you a deal.

PEARL. I can't afford it.

FRED. No problem. Have a nice day.

FRED *goes to walk away.*

PEARL. I'll give you seven hundred for the lot.

FRED. Now you're having a laugh.

JAN. Pearl, that's way too much.

PEARL. Seven hundred pounds, cash in hand.

FRED. No can do.

SHELLEY. Do you take plastic?

JAN. How much are they worth? Face value, I mean.

PEARL. Fifty.

JAN. Fifty pounds? You should be ashamed of yourself.

FRED. It's supply and demand. If you don't want 'em, there's plenty more who do.

JAN. Have you got no principles?

SHELLEY *(seductively).* Have you got somewhere we can go?

FRED. I've got a pregnant wife at home and we're skint.
Twelve hundred.

PEARL. I've only got a grand.

JAN. And you're not giving it to him, no way.

SHELLEY. I'd rather go over the wall.

FRED. In that skirt? Good luck.

He moves away.

Grandstand tickets, grandstand tickets.

Exit FRED.

SHELLEY. Tosser.

JAN. Now what?

PEARL. Well, if that's what they're charging, we might as well go home.

SHELLEY. We can't.

JAN. We don't have to. We could get ourselves a nice pub lunch.

SHELLEY. I've not got done up like this to eat scampi and chips.

JAN. Well, have you got any better ideas?

Enter LINDA, *carrying a purse.*

SHELLEY. And where have you been?

LINDA. Portaloo.

SHELLEY. All this time?

JAN. Don't take it out on her.

LINDA. I went looking for the lady who lost this.

JAN. Where d'you find it?

SHELLEY. Give it here.

SHELLEY *takes the purse.*

LINDA. She left it in the toilet. I tried to track her down. She had a hat on like a wedding cake.

PEARL. We've seen her.

JAN. She walked past us.

LINDA. Which way?

PEARL. Down there. Just a minute ago.

SHELLEY. Look at this.

LINDA. Shall I go after her?

SHELLEY. There's cash and cards and . . .

PEARL. What?

SHELLEY. Linda, you cracker! You little diamond, you.

LINDA. What?

SHELLEY *pulls out four tickets.*

SHELLEY. Tickets. Four tickets.

JAN. We'd better go and find her. She can't get in without 'em.

SHELLEY. You're right. But we can.

PEARL. Oh no . . .

SHELLEY. Oh yes. Oh yes!!!

PEARL. But they don't belong to us.

SHELLEY. They do now.

JAN. That's stealing.

SHELLEY. No, it's fate.

LINDA. I tried to find her, honest I did.

PEARL. We know that, luv.

SHELLEY. And we can hand in the purse. She'll get her cash and cards back at least.

JAN. But what if we get caught?

SHELLEY. We won't.

JAN. It's wrong.

SHELLEY. Wrong? It's a stroke of good luck for once in our lives. I mean, when was the last time we had a break?

JAN. Dunno.

PEARL. A long time ago.

LINDA. Never.

SHELLEY. There's more cash in here than we earn in a month. It's a Robin Hood thing, in't it? Get in.

SHELLEY *pockets the purse and ushers PEARL, JAN and LINDA into the racecourse.*

Scene Four

Enclosure. Moments later. JIM McCORMACK, a TV pundit, is presenting to camera. PEARL, JAN, LINDA and SHELLEY are watching him.

JIM. And welcome one and all to day three of Royal Ascot at York; a week of spectacular pageantry, stylish outfits, top hospitality and horse racing of the highest order.

PEARL. Look, it's him off the telly.

JAN. What's his name?

SHELLEY. Who cares, he's gross.

JAN. Jim, in't it?

PEARL. Jim McCormack.

JIM. With its sleek lean horses and marvellous millinery, bright silks and roaring crowds, Royal Ascot is one of the most colourful and popular events of the British summer season.

LINDA. Can I take my hat off?

SHELLEY. No.

LINDA. It's itchy.

SHELLEY. Beauty is pain.

JIM. And as well as the pageantry, Royal Ascot is known as a fashion catwalk *par excellence*. It may be the sport of kings, but Ascot holds a strong appeal for almost everyone, be they here for horses or hats, isn't that right, madam?

JIM turns the microphone to SHELLEY.

SHELLEY. Yeh.

JIM. And your name is?

Beat.

SHELLEY. Sahara.

JAN. Sahara?

JIM. So what brought you to Royal Ascot, Sahara?

SHELLEY. The bus.

JIM. And is this your first Ladies' Day?

SHELLEY. Oh no, I come every week, me. I know everyone.

JIM. Right. And do you have a tip for us?

SHELLEY. A tip?

JIM. Yes please.

PEARL. Wait for it.

SHELLEY. Don't mix your drinks.

JIM. Good . . . and as the years go by, the quality of horse racing action at Royal Ascot remains unsurpassed. Let's take a look at the race card today.

    JIM *comes off air and has a crafty drink from his hip flask.*

JAN. Well, if you're Sahara, does that mean I'm Gobi?

PEARL. Am I Kalahari?

SHELLEY. Lots of people in showbiz change their name.

JAN. But you're not in showbiz.

SHELLEY. I was just then.

LINDA. Can we go and see the horses?

JAN. 'What brought you to Royal Ascot, Sahara?'

PEARL. 'The bus.'

SHELLEY. You can laugh all you like, I could get spotted from that.

    LINDA *pulls out a bag of sugar lumps.*

LINDA. I've bought 'em these.

JAN. You can't feed 'em, Linda.

LINDA. It's only a sugar lump.

JAN. They're racehorses, they're on diets.

LINDA. Oh.

LINDA *feeds herself a sugar lump.*

SHELLEY. Linda, you're in high society now.

LINDA. I'm hungry.

SHELLEY. And I need a drink.

PEARL. You're not the only one.

JAN. What did you have for your tea last night, Linda?

LINDA. Pizza.

JAN. We had spaghetti bolognese –

SHELLEY. So where are they, exactly?

JAN. Who?

SHELLEY. The rich and famous. The celebrities, the millionaires, the Beckhams.

LINDA. Tony Christie.

PEARL. Over there in the Grandstand.

SHELLEY. And where are we again?

PEARL. The enclosure.

SHELLEY. The common end?

JAN. I think it's very nice.

SHELLEY. Can't we upgrade or summat?

PEARL. We're in, what more do you want?

SHELLEY. Hang on a minute . . . I've not bought a new hat, a new dress, a new pair of shoes to spend all day rubbing shoulders with the riff-raff. I mean, I can do that at work –

JAN. Here we go. The gob's under starters orders.

SHELLEY. I thought we'd be mingling with the stars.

JIM *(hand on earpiece).* Standing by.

PEARL. You've got Jim Wotsit over there, what more do you need?

SHELLEY. Bugger Jim Wotsit. What chance have I got to pull a millionaire in here?

PEARL gives some money to SHELLEY.

PEARL. Here. A bottle of white wine and four glasses, go on.

SHELLEY. And what did your last slave die of?

PEARL. Dehydration. Off you trot.

JIM. But before the racing begins, the Royal Procession.

JAN. Ooh, let's have a look at 'em.

SHELLEY. No, ta. They're so last year.

Exit SHELLEY. PEARL, JAN and LINDA line up to see the procession.

JIM *(to camera)*. The Queen and other members of the Royal Family traditionally attend the entire five-day meeting.

PEARL. Don't she look fed up?

JAN. She's got a lot on her plate.

PEARL. I wish she'd do summat with her hair.

LINDA. I don't get the Royal Family. I don't understand.

JIM. The carriages you see are five Ascot landaus with basket-work sides, kept at the Royal Mews at Windsor Castle.

JAN. She's never put a foot wrong. *(Shouts.)* Keep your chin up, ma'am.

LINDA. I mean, what do they do? What are they for?

PEARL. Selling papers.

JAN. It's time they left 'em alone. Reporters posing as footmen. It's none of our business what the Queen has for breakfast.

PEARL. We're taxpayers, we've got a right to know.

JAN. We know too much, that's the trouble. They've lost their mystique.

PEARL. They've lost the will to live by the look of 'em.

LINDA. I think they're just lost.

JIM. As an owner and breeder, The Queen takes a keen interest in the races.

PEARL. I quite like old Charlie – with his lady at last.

JAN. Look at her sat there like the cat what got the cream.

JIM. She last won at Royal Ascot in 1995, when Phantom Gold took the Ribblesdale Stakes.

PEARL. Well, I'm glad they got wed. It's hypocritical to hide it.

JAN. She's the hypocrite. She's nowt but a high-class home-wrecker.

LINDA. Who is?

JAN. Linda, where've you been? The old blonde.

LINDA. The one who always looks embarrassed?

JAN. Ashamed, more like.

PEARL. She waited twenty years for him. That's romantic in my book.

JIM. The Royal Enclosure was established to provide the Royal Family with privacy and security.

JAN. When I think what they did to that poor girl.

PEARL. Poor my eye. She knew the score.

JIM. This was judged essential in 1832, when William IV was hit by a stone.

PEARL. And Mrs Woman's paid the price. She's had bread rolls lobbed at her in shops an' all sorts.

LINDA. By who?

JAN. Loyal subjects.

PEARL. Loonies.

JAN. It'd been a tin of beans if I were there.

JIM. Jockeys riding Her Majesty's horses can be distinguished by the Queen's racing colours.

LINDA. I was born on Royal Wedding day.

JAN. I didn't know that, Lin. What an honour.

LINDA. Me Nan kept souvenirs. A tea-towel, a copy of the paper.

JIM. Purple body, gold braid, scarlet sleeves and black velvet cap with gold fringe.

LINDA. She collected all sorts of stuff because of it. I tried to like 'em for her sake but I still can't see it.

JAN. They're an institution, Linda. The Royal Family are what makes Britain great.

LINDA. But it's not great, is it? There's all sorts of things wrong.

JAN. They embody the values we all hold dear. Or they did.

PEARL. Two people fell in love, that's all.

JAN. Two married people.

JIM. And on they go.

PEARL. Jan, there's husbands and there's happy-ever-afters. They don't always go together, you know that.

JAN. Are you comparing me to Camilla Parker-Bowles?

LINDA. Jan don't look nothing like her.

JAN. 'Cos if I'm owt, I'm a Diana.

PEARL. I'm just saying, real love in the real world, it's not like the fairytales. It's messy and painful and people get hurt.

JAN. Do you think I don't know that?

Enter SHELLEY *with a bottle of champagne and four glasses, singing.*

SHELLEY. Who wants to shag a millionaire? I do!

JAN. Louder, luv. I don't think they heard you in the Grandstand.

PEARL. Champagne?

SHELLEY. Some of us are here to enjoy ourselves.

PEARL. I only gave you a tenner.

JAN. You've not dipped into that purse, have you?

SHELLEY. She won't miss it.

LINDA. I don't like champagne.

SHELLEY. 'Course you do.

LINDA. I don't. I'd rather have a Coke.

SHELLEY. Fine. More for me.

JAN. Here you go, Lin.

> JAN *takes a can of Coke from cool bag and gives it to* LINDA.

SHELLEY. You should see the money going over that bar. Fifty pound notes and all sorts.

> PEARL *passes* JAN *a glass of champagne.*

PEARL. Jan.

JAN. Just the one. You know I'm not a drinker.

SHELLEY. We'll soon change that. Once your Claire's off your hands, you can hit the town with me.

PEARL. That I'd like to see.

SHELLEY. You can get yourself out and get a bit of you-know-what.

JAN. Who says I want it?

SHELLEY. Everybody wants it.

JAN. Actually, Shelley, that's one of the biggest myths of our time. Plenty of folk are quite happy without it.

SHELLEY. Speak for yourself.

JAN. I do, as it happens. I'm perfectly contented as I am. I can go where I want, do what I want and I don't have to answer to anyone.

SHELLEY. Come on, when was the last time you . . .

JAN. That's my business.

SHELLEY. Was it your husband?

PEARL. Shelley . . .

SHELLEY. I'm only asking.

JAN. As a matter of fact, yes, it was.

SHELLEY. And how long ago did he clear off?

JAN. Claire was four.

SHELLEY. You poor cow.

JAN. I've had a very fulfilling life, as it happens. I've raised a beautiful girl who's been the light of my life.

SHELLEY. But we all want a few fireworks every now and then.

JAN. What are fireworks? They're here one minute and gone the next. No, I've done better than that. I've put a star in the sky.

LINDA. Aaah.

SHELLEY. So how come he left you?

JAN. He didn't. I chucked him out.

SHELLEY. Why?

JAN. It was a long time ago, Shelley.

SHELLEY. Fine, if you don't want to tell us.

JAN. He changed, if you must know. From the day I fell pregnant. He had to trade in his MG and I don't think he ever forgave me. And when she were born, Rob were jealous. Imagine that? Jealous of his own little girl. He said I never paid him no attention no more but I told him, 'I'm a mother now, she has to come first.' Rob were neither use nor ornament where Claire was concerned. I couldn't leave her on her own with him, he didn't have a clue. He couldn't bath her, change her, he showed more care and concern for that Astra. Then of course, he got talking to the girl across the road. As soon as his bonnet went up, she'd be out. She was learning to drive, he said he'd take her for a spin and that were that. I tried to make it work for the sake of our Claire but in the end, we were better off without him.

LINDA. Does Claire not see him?

JAN. No. He sends money for her birthday and she won't cash the cheque. She says, 'We don't need him or his money. You're mum, dad and big sister to me.'

PEARL. Where is he now, Jan?

JAN. He got a job in Sales. Ended up as an Area Manager of summat. Company car, the works. Last thing we heard, they were in South Cave.

SHELLEY. He's rich, then?

JAN. He's done all right.

SHELLEY. I bet you wish you'd kept your trap shut now.

JAN. A million pounds couldn't replace what I've got with Claire.

SHELLEY. But come September, she'll be gone and you'll be stuck in with nowt and no one.

JAN. She'll be home for the holidays.

SHELLEY. She'll be seeing the world with her student mates and you'll be working double-shift to pay for it all.

JAN. Well, if that's what helps Claire –

SHELLEY. Sod Claire. What about you?

JAN. Are we having a toast?

PEARL. To what?

JAN. To Pearl on her retirement.

PEARL. I'm not retiring.

JAN. All right. To us.

PEARL. To mates.

PEARL/SHELLEY/JAN (*together*). Mates.

LINDA. Mates.

JIM *sidles over.*

PEARL. Ey, Jim Wotsit's back.

JAN. What's he staring at?

SHELLEY. What do you think? Me.

LINDA. How come?

SHELLEY. Because, Linda, he knows talent when he sees it.

PEARL. I bet he does.

SHELLEY *(loudly).* I've got star quality, me. I've been told.

JAN. By who?

SHELLEY. Agents. Managers. All sorts.

JAN. You work in a fish plant.

SHELLEY. So did Annie Lennox.

JAN. I mean, let's face it. We've got no qualifications, no
    nothing. What chance have we got of getting out?

JIM. Getting out of what, exactly?

SHELLEY. The enclosure. We should be in the Grandstand.

JIM. The Grandstand? I'd say your chances are . . . *(Puts fists
    on top of each other.)* Fifty to one.

SHELLEY. You what?

JIM. That's fifty to one in the tic-tac.

SHELLEY. Tic-tac?

JIM. You've seen the bookies on their pitches? Well, that's how
    they talked in the days before mobile phone. *(Moves hands
    up and down, and opens mouth.)* Levels you devils, that's
    Evens. *(Crosses hands and smiles.)* That's five to four; well
    to fancied. *(Right hand on left cheek.)* six to four; the
    ear'ole.

SHELLEY. More like arsehole.

JIM *(right hand on shoulder).* seven to four; the shoulder.
    (Hands on head.) I bet you've seen this one; nine to four.

(*Hands on nose.*) five to two. (*Waves right hand above left.*) four to one. (*Hands on both shoulders.*) nine to two. (*Right hand on shoulder and pouts.*) five to one. (*Brings fists together.*) ten to one. (*Crosses hands over chest.*) thirty-three to one. (*Puts fists on top of each other.*) fifty to one.

SHELLEY. Fascinating.

JIM. Have a go, Sahara.

SHELLEY. No, ta.

PEARL. Go on.

JAN. Go on, Sahara.

SHELLEY. All right, then. I will.

JIM (*moves hands up and down, and opens mouth*). Evens.

SHELLEY (*moves hands up and down, and opens mouth*). Evens.

JIM (*crosses hands and smiles*). Five to four.

SHELLEY (*crosses hands and smiles*). Five to four.

JIM (*right hand on left cheek*). You've got it, six to four.

SHELLEY. Six to four?

JIM. Right hand on left cheek.

   SHELLEY *puts her hand on her backside.*

   Higher, my dear.

SHELLEY. Six to four.

PEARL. She's a natural.

JAN. I'll say.

JIM (*right hand on shoulder*). Seven to four.

SHELLEY (*left hand on shoulder*). Seven to four.

PEARL. Right hand.

SHELLEY. I know. It's harder than it looks.

JIM (*hands on head*). Hands on head, nine to four.

SHELLEY (*hands on head*). Hands on head, nine to four.

JIM (*hands on nose*). Hands on nose, five to two.

SHELLEY (*hands on nose*). Hands on nose, five to two.

JIM (*waves right hand above left*). Right hand above left, four to one.

SHELLEY (*waves left hand above right*). Four to one.

JAN. Wrong.

JIM (*hands on both shoulders*). Try again, nine to two.

SHELLEY (*hands on both shoulders*). Nine to two.

JIM (*right hand on shoulder and pouts*). That's it, five to one.

SHELLEY (*right hand on shoulder and pouts*). Five to one.

LINDA. She's gerrin' it now.

JIM (*brings fists together*). Fists together, ten to one.

SHELLEY (*brings fists together*). Right.

JIM (*crosses hands over chest*). Hands on chest, thirty-three to one.

SHELLEY (*crosses hands over chest*). Is that it?

JIM. Perfect. (*Fists on top of each other*). Both fists together, fifty to one. Bravo!

LINDA. Can we have a go?

SHELLEY. That's enough now.

JIM. No, come on.

Following JIM*'s lead, they try again.* JIM *speeds it up.*

(*Moves hands up and down, and opens mouth.*) Evens.

ALL (*moves hands up and down, and opens mouth*). Evens.

JIM (*crosses hands and smiles*). Five to four.

ALL (*crosses hands and smiles*). Five to four.

JIM (*right hand on left cheek*). Six to four.

ALL (*right hand on left cheek*). Six to four.

JIM (*right hand on shoulder*). Seven to four.

ALL (*right hand on shoulder*). Seven to four.

JIM (*hands on head*). Nine to four.

ALL (*hands on head*). Nine to four.

JIM (*hands on nose*). Five to two.

ALL (*hands on nose*). Five to two.

JIM. Christ! (*To camera.*) Hello and welcome back to Royal Ascot. And thank you to the Hull and District Hand-Jiving Club. Take a bow, girls.

SHELLEY *bows,* LINDA *looks terrified,* JAN *mouths 'Hello Claire' and* PEARL *waves to the camera.*

Coming up is the first race of the day, the two thirty Norfolk Stakes. First run in 1843, it's now one of the first group races of the season for juveniles and provides a real test of speed for promising two-year-olds. Let's have a look at the runners and riders.

PEARL. Good thinking.

JIM. Ladies, I'll be back.

PEARL *takes a copy of the* Racing Post *from her bag.*

SHELLEY. Isn't he professional?

PEARL. That's one way of putting it.

JAN. Racing Post? You've come prepared.

PEARL. Mick got it for me this morning.

SHELLEY. Are we having a bet then?

JAN. Just a flutter.

LINDA. Are we having dinner?

JAN. All right, Linda. Here you go.

JAN *passes around the sandwiches.*

PEARL. Right then. In the two thirty Norfolk Stakes, we've got Golden Storm at five to one; Purple Spirit, five to one; Gemini Diamond five to two; Tony's Lad, four to one.

LINDA. Like Tony Christie.

PEARL. Sweet Gypsy Rose three to one.

JAN. It's all Japanese to me.

PEARL. It's not really. Put a quid on a three to one, you'll get three back if it wins. Put two quid on a five to two, you win a fiver, it's simple.

JAN. So do you pick 'em at random?

SHELLEY. You've got to study the form, an't yer? Everyone knows that.

PEARL. Go on, then.

SHELLEY. What?

PEARL. Study it.

PEARL *hands the* Racing Post *to* SHELLEY.

SHELLEY (*reads*). 'Sweet Gypsy Rose hit a rich vein when landing a couple of firm ground handicaps with eye shield in May. Looks the one to beat in current fettle, despite slight concerns regarding today's longer trip.'

JAN. Right . . .

SHELLEY (*reads*). 'Purple Spirit; Useful/consistent up to 7f on turf last year but below that level in two starts this term; good chance strictly on ratings and worth a try over 1m.'

JAN. Okay . . .

SHELLEY. See?

LINDA. Jan?

JAN. What?

LINDA. These sandwiches are nice.

JAN. Good.

PEARL. A bookie don't set odds by owt as fickle as form, not if he wants to make money.

JAN. So what does he do?

JAN *cracks open a hard-boiled egg.*

PEARL. It's pure mathematics. Say you put a hundred quid on Sweet Gypsy Rose at three to one. If you win, the bookie pays you £300, that's the deal. They've got to set that £300 against everything else so they'll juggle the odds until they've taken more than any horse pays out. They'll drop, say, Golden Storm to two to one and raise the prices on the others. Go from five to two to four to one on Gemini Diamond, raise Sweet Gypsy Rose to four to one. They'll get to the point where it doesn't matter who wins, they've taken enough to pay out and make a profit. So the bookie always wins in the end.

SHELLEY. Perhaps we'll pick 'em by the colours.

PEARL. Well, shall we do the Jackpot on the Tote?

JAN. The what?

PEARL. See that big betting shop over there? That's the Tote. It's run by the government, believe it or not. All the profits go back into racing.

SHELLEY. So we don't go to one of them bookies on the stands?

PEARL. Not for the Jackpot. It's a national thing, you know? Like the Lottery.

LINDA. I won a tenner on the Lottery last week.

JAN. Lucky Linda.

PEARL. The Tote picks a race card for the Jackpot every day. You have a bet on six races and the money gets pooled. Pick the winner of all six and you win the national pot.

SHELLEY. How much is that?

PEARL. Well, it's a rollover, Mick says. Near-on half a million.

SHELLEY. You're kidding?

JAN. How much do you bet, then?

PEARL. Perhaps a quid each, that's all.

SHELLEY. Sod a quid, let's bet a grand. You've got it in your bag.

JAN. That's her rainy day fund.

SHELLEY. She'll be sunning herself in the Maldives if it comes in.

JAN. And if we lose on the first race?

PEARL. Okay – why don't we bet a fiver each? We'd get a bigger percentage if they all came in.

SHELLEY. Last of the big spenders.

PEARL. It's just a bit of fun, in't it? Right then, ladies. Let's go to the Tote and put our money where our mouth is.

JAN. Shouldn't someone keep our seats?

PEARL. Jan, we've not come to Ascot to sit in the beer tent all day.

SHELLEY. We've got to find Beckham.

LINDA. And Tony.

JAN. If I knew we'd be walking, I'd have worn my other shoes.

SHELLEY. You've got no sense of adventure, you.

JAN. My feet are killing me.

SHELLEY. Have another drink, you won't feel 'em.

PEARL. Champagne again?

JAN. All right, just the one.

SHELLEY. Shall we get another bottle on the way?

PEARL. Why not?

Exit all, singing the Amarillo sha-la-la's.

Scene Five

Racecourse. Two hours later. Enter JIM McCORMACK, *talking to camera.*

JIM. To update you on the Jackpot, today's win pool is £543,223. There's over six thousand tickets sold with four legs to go. And they're lining up now for one of the biggest races of the day. Founded in 1807, the Gold Cup is the oldest and one of the most prestigious races at Royal Ascot. Staged over the marathon trip of two-and-a-half miles, the race is a stiff test of stamina and attracts the very best staying horses.

From offstage, we hear the women singing 'Avenues and Alleyways' by Tony Christie.

Many have distinguished themselves with multiple Gold Cup wins, enhancing the race's reputation as a specialist's event. Blind Alley'll be looking for his third consecutive win and if he can rattle and roll early on, he should do well. Tory Boy battled to win the last two times, he likes to run close to the pace and he's well drawn to do so. Bearded Lady looked well in the paddock, he's been getting a little bit sweaty later on in the proceedings but he won at Haydock which is promising.

Enter PEARL, LINDA, SHELLEY *and* JAN. *All but* LINDA *carry a champagne bottle. They are singing drunkenly.*

Ladies, please.

SHELLEY. Sorry.

The women giggle and 'shhh' each other as JIM *continues his broadcast.*

JIM. Last Supper looks well, won once this season but very consistent and a far weaker race would suit him. Chimney's At Dusk is nicely drawn in stall four but Last Chance Saloon, let's be clear, he's been done no favours at all.

SHELLEY. What's he on about?

PEARL. Who cares? We've won.

JAN. Twice.

SHELLEY *raises her bottle.*

SHELLEY. To . . . ? What was its name again?

PEARL. Tony's Lad.

PEARL/JAN/LINDA/SHELLEY. Tony's Lad.

SHELLEY. And who was the next one?

PEARL. Solitaire.

PEARL/JAN/LINDA/SHELLEY. Solitaire.

JIM. So you're celebrating, ladies?

SHELLEY. We're on a winning streak.

JIM. Beginner's luck, ey?

LINDA. How come they've all got stupid names?

JIM. They're not stupid at all, my dear. In fact, there's strict rules that govern naming.

JAN. Here we go, lesson two.

JIM. The Jockey Club states that names must consist of no more than eighteen letters, must not use initials or numerals, trade names, names of notorious people, titles of copyright books, films or plays, or names that are suggestive, vulgar or obscene.

LINDA. Oh.

SHELLEY. So you couldn't call it Big –

JIM. Some names are chosen because they imply a horse is powerful, others have a touch of humour and many get their names from their mother. Dinner Time's foal was Eight Thirty, for example.

LINDA. Why?

JIM. Well, dinner time's eight thirty, is it not?

LINDA. I have mine at twelve.

JIM. Well then, if you had a horse, you'd call it Twelve.

LINDA. No, I wouldn't. I'd call it Christie.

JIM. Are you being facetious?

LINDA. I don't know.

JIM. Well my dear, I suggest you go away and come back when you do.

Exit JIM.

LINDA. What does he mean?

JAN. Nothing. He thinks he's a cut above us just 'cos he's on the telly.

SHELLEY. He's a professional.

JAN. That's a matter of opinion. Who've we got in the next race?

PEARL. Blind Alley. Then it's Sweet Maria, Reno or Bust and Broken Dreams.

JAN. All from the songs of you-know-who, ey Lin?

LINDA. He shouldn't speak to us like that. It's not my fault, I've done nothing wrong.

SHELLEY. We know, get over it.

JAN. Leave her.

SHELLEY. She's pissed him off, an't she? He won't talk to us now.

JAN. I thought you thought he was gross?

PEARL. Are you all right, Linda?

LINDA. Yeh.

PEARL. Are you sure?

LINDA. Course.

SHELLEY. Well, cheer up then. Stick a rum in your Coke.

LINDA. I've drunk it, can I have another?

JAN. I'm sorry luv, you've had the lot.

LINDA. Oh.

SHELLEY. Go to the bar and get one.

LINDA. You're all right.

SHELLEY. Go on, you tight-arse.

LINDA. I've changed my mind. I don't want one.

SHELLEY. You just said you did.

PEARL. Don't get on to her.

SHELLEY. Go and get yourself a Coke.

LINDA. I can't.

PEARL. Course you can, it's just round the corner.

LINDA. I can't. I've lost my purse.

JAN. When?

PEARL. You had it at the Tote.

LINDA. I must have dropped it.

PEARL. Oh aye.

JAN. Again?

LINDA. Like that lady in the loo.

SHELLEY. Let's double-check, shall we?

SHELLEY *grabs* LINDA*'s handbag.*

LINDA. Don't.

SHELLEY. Panic over, we've found it.

LINDA. Oh yeh.

SHELLEY. And quelle surprise, it's empty.

LINDA. I had a tenner but I spent it on the bus.

PEARL. So what have you been buying?

LINDA. Nowt.

PEARL. Are you sure about that?

LINDA. Yeh.

JAN. So how come you're skint?

LINDA. I just am, that's all.

Beat.

JAN. Has she been round again?

LINDA. No.

SHELLEY. She's lying.

PEARL. Has she, Linda?

LINDA. I told you, no.

PEARL. Has she?

LINDA. Yeh.

JAN. Linda!

LINDA. I'm just helping her out. She's got nowhere else to go.

JAN. She's not sleeping on your sofa, is she?

LINDA. No.

JAN. Is she?

LINDA. No.

JAN. Good.

LINDA. I've given her the bed.

SHELLEY. Are you for real?

JAN. Why do you do it, Linda? After everything we've said?

LINDA. I want to help her, that's all.

PEARL. So when did she turn up?

LINDA. Not long ago. Last night.

PEARL. And she's already had her hand in your purse?

LINDA. I just borrowed her some.

PEARL. So what's the story this time?

LINDA. Her bloke chucked her out. She's just stopping wi'me til she gets back on her feet.

PEARL. She said that last time, remember?

JAN. And the time before that.

PEARL. She ate your food, drank your drink and ran up three hundred quid on the phone.

LINDA. It weren't that much.

PEARL. And what happened to that perfume we bought you for your birthday? What?

LINDA. Dunno.

PEARL. Well, shall I remind you? She sold it down the pub for twenty quid.

LINDA. No, she never.

PEARL. Linda, I was there with Mick, I saw her.

LINDA. She's all right underneath.

JAN. And was she all right underneath when she moved in with you? Or did she chuck you out and nick your bloke?

LINDA. She didn't chuck me out, I left.

PEARL. Did she nick your bloke?

LINDA. Leave me alone.

JAN. She's trouble, Lin.

SHELLEY. She's scum.

LINDA. She's my mum!

Beat.

PEARL. I know she is. I know. We're just concerned for you, that's all.

JAN. We've been here so many times, Lin.

SHELLEY. She doesn't give a toss, you should know that by now.

LINDA. Shut up – you don't understand – leave me alone.

Exit LINDA.

PEARL. Linda?

JAN. Linda!

PEARL. Bloody hell fire.

JAN. Nice one, Shelley!

SHELLEY. Well, it's true.

PEARL. You don't have to rub it in her face, though.

SHELLEY. You'd better go after her.

JAN. You go.

SHELLEY. She'll be back.

PEARL. For God's sake, Shelley, just do as you're told for once and go!

Exit SHELLEY.

JAN. What's up?

PEARL. Nothing ever changes. It's the same old story, no matter what you say or do.

JAN. You've done plenty for the pair of them.

PEARL. Have I? Sometimes, I think I've done nowt with my life.

JAN. You're a wife, a mother, a good mate. I'd say that counts for something?

PEARL. I know you would.

JAN. So what's the problem?

PEARL. I'm all right.

JAN. We've been friends for twenty years, Pearl. I know you, come on?

PEARL. I've had too much to drink.

JAN. You and me both.

PEARL. I've had too much to drink and I'm gonna tell you summat but you've got to promise me, you'll keep it to yourself.

JAN. I will.

PEARL. I mean it, Jan. You can't breathe a word of it to no one.

JAN. What is it? Have you bumped someone off?

PEARL. I've got a lover.

JAN. No, come on, what is it?

PEARL. I've got a lover.

Beat.

JAN. You're not joking, are you?

PEARL. I wish I was.

JAN. A lover? At your age? You're practically a pensioner.

PEARL. Perhaps we'll talk about this another time?

JAN. Oh no, I wanna talk about it now. What's his name?

PEARL. Jan –

JAN. Come on, do I know him?

PEARL. No.

JAN. So what's his name?

PEARL. Barry.

JAN. And where did you meet him?

PEARL. At the Station Hotel. Kelly's wedding reception.

JAN. But that's –

PEARL. I know. Seven years ago this month – and I can't tell you how good it is to say it out loud.

JAN. But I was there . . . I don't remember . . . what happened?

PEARL. After the punch-up, I went through to the lounge and sat there on me tod thinking 'What's it all about?' You lot

are staggering round the dance floor to Hi-Ho Silver Lining,
I'm looking in me bag to find my phone to call a cab. Next
thing I know, there's a glass of white wine on my table. The
waiter says it's from the fella at the bar. Room one two four.
I look up and the fella looks back and summat clicks,
summat like you only see in films.

JAN. Bloody hell.

PEARL. I raised me glass to say 'ta' and he gives us a nod and
it was just like . . . I dunno, like I'd known him forever . . .
but I'd never known owt like it. My hands are shaking so
much, I can hardly hold the glass. He gets up from the bar,
looks, goes to the lift . . . and so do I.

JAN. With him?

PEARL. Of course with him.

JAN. But he could have been a psycho.

PEARL. He could have but he weren't.

JAN. So what did he say when you got there?

PEARL. Nowt.

JAN. What? You just sat there?

PEARL. No.

JAN. So what happened?

PEARL. Do I have to spell it out?

JAN. You never?

PEARL. We did. 'Til five in the morning.

JAN. And what was it like?

PEARL. Paradise.

JAN. But one night of passion can't match what you've got.

PEARL. It weren't one night.

JAN. You what?

PEARL. He comes up on business. I go to the Station and I
meet him in the room. We have a meal sent up. A bottle of

wine or two. He always buys me chocolates, them proper ones from Thorntons. And we talk and talk and talk.

JAN. And where do you tell Mick you are?

PEARL. At yours.

JAN. Oh, do you now?

PEARL. I'm sorry Jan. I know I should have told you but I didn't want to ask you to lie.

JAN. What if Mick had rung me up?

PEARL. I thought, 'Well, if he does, I'll deal with it then.' And in a way, I hoped he would.

JAN. I thought I knew you, Pearl. I thought we told each other everything.

PEARL. We do but they were the rules. Me and him, we agreed on 'em right at the beginning. If we want to keep it going then we had to have rules.

JAN. Like what?

PEARL. Don't tell a soul, no matter how much you trust 'em. Don't be seen together outside the room. No addresses, no phone numbers, no surnames. We're just Barry and Pearl in one two four.

JAN. Is he married an' all?

PEARL. He is, yeh.

JAN. I thought as much.

PEARL. And I know it's wrong but he's the one thing I do for myself. Or he was.

JAN. How do you mean?

PEARL. Three months ago, I turned up at the Station as arranged. The room was booked. He never came. I went back the next night and waited in the lounge. I sat there every night for a week. Nowt. I don't know what's gone off.

JAN. Well, it's obvious. He's dumped you and he hasn't got the decency to tell you to your face.

PEARL. He wouldn't just walk away, I know him.

JAN. I bet his wife said the same.

PEARL. But I know he wouldn't just not come.

JAN. So what are you gonna do? Turn up at the Station every night 'til Kingdom Come? You can't sit in a hotel bar, a woman on your own. They'll think you're a –

PEARL. I don't care what they think, I just want a reason. I just want to find him.

JAN. Well, there's not much chance of that if you don't know his name.

PEARL. He's a bookie. He works all over the country. He always does Ascot, he's bought himself a pitch. He'll be in amongst 'em over there, I know he will.

JIM (*voiceover*). They're lining up now for three forty-five Gold Cup . . . and they're off! First away is Park Drive, followed by Last Supper, Blue Cheese Soup with Bearded Lady coming up on the inside.

JAN. Rainy day money, ey?

PEARL. Yeh. And it's been siling it down since he went.

JAN. So is that's why you've come? To get him back.

PEARL. Maybe. I don't know.

JAN. Pearl, you're married. You've got four kids and a grandson and a house all bought and paid for and a caravan in Patrington Haven and now you're chucking it all away –

PEARL. Who says?

JAN. All right, you've had a fling, your bit of fun but you're a wife and a mother.

PEARL. I'm still me though. I'm still . . .

JAN. What?

PEARL. I'm all the things you say I am but that's not all I am. You understand that, don't you?

JAN. Forget him.

PEARL. I can't.

JAN. Forget him.

PEARL. I don't want to.

JAN. So you want to leave Mick? Do you?

PEARL. That weren't in the rules.

JAN. So what do you want?

PEARL. Just to see him one more time. Just to know.

JIM (*voiceover*). Last Supper in the lead now, followed by
    Blind Alley. As they head into the final furlong, it's Last
    Supper from Blind Alley, and Bearded Lady in third place
    has unseated his rider. It's Last Supper with Blind Alley
    coming up on the inside, they're neck and neck, Blind Alley
    pushes through and it's Blind Alley from Last Supper. Blind
    Alley wins the Gold Cup. Blind Alley!

PEARL. That's us.

JAN. Must be our lucky day.

PEARL. I had my reasons, luv.

JAN. I daresay. You'll find me in the bar.

    Exit JAN. PEARL *takes out a compact and retouches her
    lipstick. She takes a last look in the mirror and snaps it shut.*

ACT TWO

Scene One

Paddock. One hour later. PATRICK, an Irish jockey, dressed in full racing silks, is having a cigarette.

PATRICK (*gestures to his cigarette*). Yes, I know I'm an athlete. And I know it's probably gonna kill me in the end but I'm hungry. I'm so feckin' hungry I could eat that feckin' horse. You can't live on coffee and a dry piece of toast, and I don't mean just for breakfast, for the whole feckin' day. No, for the last feckin' twenty-five years. You think I'm joking? Most fellas shut their eyes and dream of Paris Hilton. My fantasies are fry-ups and freshly-baked bread but they won't let me earn a living if I'm over eight stone four. Eight stone four, what kind of weight is that for a grown man? What kind of feckin' life? But we don't say that, do we? At least not to the press or the public. We don't talk about that one meal a day and all those hours in the sauna, the gym, the toilet. We don't talk about the laxatives and locker-room vomiting and –

Enter LINDA, singing the Amarillo 'sha-la-la's'.

You can't come in here, Miss. Not without a badge.

LINDA. I've got a badge.

LINDA shows PATRICK the badge she's wearing.

PATRICK. Let's have a look, now. The Tony Christie Fan Club.

LINDA. He's come here today, Shelley says.

PATRICK. Shelley?

LINDA. Me workmate. Have you seen him?

PATRICK. Not unless he's riding in the four fifteen.

LINDA. Sorry. I just want to talk to him, that's all.

PATRICK. What about?

Beat.

LINDA. Nothing much. I'd best . . .

PATRICK. So what do you do, you and Shelley?

LINDA. We pack fish in 'Ezzle.

PATRICK. 'Ezzle?

LINDA. Hull.

PATRICK. And do you like it?

LINDA. No one likes it.

PATRICK. Clocking in and clocking out. Sounds like a good craic to me.

LINDA. Are you a rider?

PATRICK. Well, how d'you guess?

LINDA. Your blouse. I like it. I like the stars.

PATRICK. They should give us one with arrows on next.

LINDA. Why?

PATRICK. Ah, take no notice. I'm just feeling sorry for myself.

LINDA. Me an' all.

PATRICK. A pretty girl like you? What have you got to worry you?

LINDA. Not much. Just stuff. I'd better go.

PATRICK. You know, my mammy liked a bit of Tony Christie.

LINDA. Yeh? My nan had all his records. She brought me up 'cos me mam weren't no good. She'd play 'em every Sunday when she made us dinner. She'd be singing with the windows all steamed up.

PATRICK. I bet she's dancing round the kitchen now he's back.

LINDA. Not really.

Beat.

PATRICK. Oh. I'm sorry.

LINDA. She had a blood clot. She should have gone to the doctors but she didn't.

PATRICK. I lost me mammy last year but I couldn't get home. The bastards had me racing in Dubai.

LINDA. Don't you like it, then? Racing.

PATRICK. Would you? I'm up at six every morning, even Sunday. Ride a couple of lots, get your weight down in the sauna, put your saddles in the car and hit the road. Two meetings a day, six races a meet, seven days a week and the only break you get is when your mount throws you off.

LINDA. Have you been thrown off?

PATRICK. Me? You couldn't count how many broken bones I've had. Last year, I was riding here at York and a great big black bird crossed the track. My horse reared up and came down on top of me. Smashed my ribs, my collarbone, my shinbone, my nose and collapsed one of my lungs for good measure.

LINDA. What about the horse?

PATRICK. Broke his leg. They shot him and do you know what? Sometimes, I wish they'd done the same to me.

LINDA. If they had, you'd not be talking to me.

PATRICK. Well, that's true enough. I'm Patrick.

LINDA. Linda.

PATRICK. Delighted to make your acquaintance, Linda.

LINDA. Ta.

PATRICK. And that's a very lovely smile you've got there.

LINDA. As if.

PATRICK. It reminds me of a girl I knew back home.

LINDA. Get lost.

PATRICK. Hey, you're not going shy on me, are you?

LINDA. No.

She laughs.

PATRICK. You've got a lovely laugh there, too.

LINDA. Stop it.

PATRICK. I'm just giving you a compliment, what's wrong with that?

Beat.

LINDA. I should go and find my friends. They'll be worried, I . . .

PATRICK. Ah, you're all right for a minute. Please? I never get the chance to talk to someone like you.

LINDA. What do you mean like me?

PATRICK. Tell me about yourself. Tell me all about your life.

LINDA. There's nowt to say.

PATRICK. I bet you've got a young man you can boast about?

LINDA. Not really.

PATRICK. A sweet lass like you? Ah, you must have.

LINDA. If you listen to the girls at work, a fella's nowt but trouble.

PATRICK. So what do you do with yourself? Come on . . .

LINDA. Well . . . I get up. Go to work. Come home. Have tea. Watch telly. Sometimes, I go with Shelley to a concert or a club but it never works out like it's supposed to. Come back. Go to bed. Get up. Go to work.

PATRICK. You know what, Linda? I'd give everything I've got . . . which isn't much, I'll grant yer . . . for that.

LINDA. For what? We've got nowt.

PATRICK. You've got friends.

LINDA. Haven't you?

PATRICK. Winners and losers, that's what this game's about. And if you're not a winner, you're nobody.

LINDA. Have you never been a winner?

PATRICK. I was once upon a time. Oh, yeah.

LINDA. What was it like?

PATRICK. I'm twenty-one years old. Reins in one hand, mane in another and a great big ugly knot in my stomach. It's taken everything I've got to come this far but I know this is just the beginning. Balanced in the stirrups, I'm ready to spring. The bell rings, the gate flies open and we're off. Shout to the horse to get him on his way, pump down on his neck to drive him on. Look around to see we're third in the pack. Raise up off the stirrups, push the mount but not too hard, there's still a long way to go. Hear the hoof beats of the horses, see their shadows on the ground and go, go, go, go, pushing through the pack. Into the Far Turn and it's high-speed chess. Crouch down in the stirrups, shorten your hold on the reins, knuckle up and down the neck to push him on. Nerves are forgotten and everything I've learned is coming good. Take the two ahead and you're top of the pack. Into the Stretch Run and break out the whip. 'Come on, come on, give us all you've got.' Body moving with the motion of the horse, and I'm pushing, pushing, pushing! Hooves on the inside, he's got to give you more. Wave the whip by his head, press down on his neck, ride him hard, hard, hard, you're fast, you're free, you're first past the post!

LINDA. Wow.

PATRICK. You take all the spills and you get back in the saddle. But then one day, you come off and you can't get back up. You've got to ride again 'cos what else can you do but you've changed. You've lost your nerve. You're scared.

LINDA. I'm scared an' all sometimes. I'm scared of my mum.

PATRICK. Why?

LINDA. Don't tell the others.

PATRICK. I don't know the others.

LINDA. They think I should stand up to her. I've tried to but she says things.

PATRICK. What kind of things?

LINDA. Nasty things.

PATRICK. Well, you shouldn't let her.

LINDA. I know but every time she comes back, I think, 'She's changed. She'll be nice this time.'

PATRICK. She's back now, is she?

LINDA. Yeh.

PATRICK. And is she being nice to you?

LINDA. No.

PATRICK. So why d'you let her in?

LINDA. 'Cos she's my mam. And I get lonely.

PATRICK. You're not the only one.

LINDA. You an' all?

PATRICK. Oh yeh – and I'm so feckin' hungry I could die.

LINDA *offers* PATRICK *a sugar lump.*

LINDA. Here. I bought 'em for the horses but they're not allowed.

PATRICK. Nor am I.

LINDA. Ah, go on.

PATRICK. I can't, I've got to race.

LINDA. When?

PATRICK. Five thirty. Broken Dreams.

LINDA. That's our horse. After 'Street of Broken Dreams', that's ours. I picked 'em all from the songs of Tony Christie.

PATRICK. Then I'll ride it for you, Linda.

LINDA *offers* PATRICK *the bag once again.*

LINDA. Please?

PATRICK. I wish I could.

LINDA. It's only a sugar lump, what's wrong with yer?

LINDA *eats a sugar lump.*

PATRICK. Ah, what the hell.

PATRICK *eats a sugar lump.*

LINDA. Well?

Beat.

PATRICK. Sweet.

Scene Two

Beer Tent. Same time. Enter JAN, drinking white wine from a pint glass. She listens to the commentary on the fourth race.

JIM (*voiceover*). Sweet Maria on the inside, forging ahead from Evil Twin and Glitterati. Sweet Maria is right out in front and as they head to the post, it's a magnificent race for Sweet Maria, four lengths ahead; the Brittania Stakes goes to Sweet Maria!

JAN. Thass us! We've wun agen! We've wun!

Enter SHELLEY.

SHELLEY. Jan?

JAN. Shell! Ave bin lookin' all ovver fur yew.

SHELLEY. What's going on?

JAN. Wezz Linda?

SHELLEY. I dunno, I can't find her. You're steaming.

JAN. I know where Purl is.

SHELLEY. How many have you had?

JAN. I've 'ad an 'ole bottle of summat burrit dun't matter duz it? Iss Laydez Daaay!

SHELLEY. Shut it.

JAN. Come 'ere, I wanna tell yer summat. I wanna wispa.

SHELLEY. What?

JAN. You're mi bezt mate you are.

SHELLEY. No, I'm not.

JAN. Yez, y'are.

SHELLEY. You don't even like me, you're always gerrin' at me.

JAN. When? When do I gerra' you?

SHELLEY. Stop breathin' in me face.

JAN. Shell?

SHELLEY. What?

JAN. I luvv you.

SHELLEY. Piss off.

JAN. Shell? I feel sick.

SHELLEY. Sit down. Stick your head between your legs, go on.

SHELLEY *shoves* JAN's *head between her legs.*

Is that better?

JAN. No.

SHELLEY. It will be. Sit.

JAN. Shell?

SHELLEY. What?

JAN. Are yer still there?

SHELLEY. No, I've buggered off.

JAN. They all buggered off an' left me too.

SHELLEY. They'll be back.

JAN. Rob left me.

SHELLEY. I thought you kicked him out.

JAN. I begged 'im to stay for the sake of our Claire but 'e left me fur hur. Rob went and now Claire –

SHELLEY. You'll be all right without her, you'll be free.

JAN. She's bin me life.

SHELLEY. And now you've got to make a new 'un.

JAN. Who with?

SHELLEY. I dunno, the world's your lobster.

JAN. But he's goin' an all.

SHELLEY. Who?

JAN. Joe.

SHELLEY. Joe from work?

JAN. He's goin' to Oztraila.

SHELLEY. Yeh, so?

JAN. He's goin' bur I want 'im to stay.

SHELLEY. Why?

JAN. Cuz I want 'im. I want 'im to stay cuz I want 'im.

SHELLEY. Jan?!

JAN (*shouts*). I want 'im.

SHELLEY. And how long has this been going on?

JAN. I's not going on, that's the trubble.

SHELLEY. Does he know how you feel?

JAN. Well, he kissed us.

SHELLEY. When?

JAN. In the taxi coming home from Kelly's wedding.

SHELLEY. Frigging hell, it all happened that night.

JAN. Then he asked us on a date an' I wanted to, I really, really wanted to but I couldn't.

SHELLEY. Why not?

JAN. 'Cos of Claire. And ever since, well, I've looked at 'im and e's looked at me an' once he was comin' through the canteen door as I was going out and he touched me accidental and Shell, I thought I'd die.

SHELLEY. Hang on – rewind – what do you mean 'cos of Claire'?

JAN. An' at the Christmas Party, we sat talkin' in a corner an' he told me all about Oztraila and he says, 'If there's owt worth staying round here for, I would,' and I says, 'Well, there's not,' when I wanted to say, 'There's me. There's me.'

SHELLEY. Yeh; what do you mean, ' 'cos of Claire'?

JAN. I mean it's not right. It's teenage girls who have the boyfriends, not their mothers.

SHELLEY. Jan, get real. You're still a woman.

JAN (*miserably*). I know.

SHELLEY. And she'll be gone in a couple of months.

JAN. So will Joe.

SHELLEY. Well, maybe not, if you tell him how you feel.

JAN. I can't.

SHELLEY. Why not? What's stopping you? Come on, what?

Beat.

JAN. Why aren't you tekking the piss?

SHELLEY. You what?

JAN. You tek the piss outta me all the time. Why aren't you doing it now?

Enter PEARL.

PEARL. Have you found Linda?

SHELLEY. No.

PEARL. Bloody hell, now what?

JAN. 'Ave you found 'im?

PEARL. What's up with her?

SHELLEY. What does it look like?

JAN. 'Ave yer?

PEARL. Do you think we should go to Missing Persons?

JAN. 'Ave ya found your Barry?

SHELLEY. Who?

PEARL. Take no notice, she's pissed.

JAN. Pearl's bin 'avin an affair wi' a bookie for seven 'ole years an' she meets 'im once a week a'the Station 'otel but you can't say owt – ssshhhh – 'cos it's a really, really, really big secret.

PEARL. That's the white wine talking.

SHELLEY. Is it?

JAN. And he's come here today, she's been to look for him and –

    JAN *slowly passes out.*

SHELLEY. Pearl?

PEARL. So now you know.

SHELLEY. But you're the last one I expected. You're happy, you're sorted.

PEARL. Yeh, I've got it all, me.

SHELLEY. Dead right you have. Go, girl!

PEARL. All right.

SHELLEY. You mucky cow.

PEARL. It's not like that.

SHELLEY. So what is it like?

PEARL. He's just someone I can talk to.

SHELLEY. Is he fit?

PEARL. Yeh.

SHELLEY. Is he rich?

PEARL. Not really.

SHELLEY. You don't love him, do you?

Beat.

PEARL. That's a big question.

SHELLEY. Do you?

PEARL. Perhaps I do, perhaps I don't. It doesn't matter now.

SHELLEY. Why?

PEARL. 'Cos he's not here, is he? I've looked everywhere.
He's gone.

SHELLEY. Friggin' hell, you two. I thought it was only me
who messed up.

PEARL. You don't do so bad.

SHELLEY. No? You don't know the half of it.

PEARL. Well, why don't you tell us?

SHELLEY. Where the frig is that Linda?

PEARL. We could help, if you let us.

Beat.

SHELLEY. You stop here with Jan, I'll have another look.

PEARL. Shelley?

SHELLEY. I'm all right. Well, I will be when I've found me
that millionaire, ey?

SHELLEY *turns to go.*

PEARL. Shell?

SHELLEY. What?

PEARL. Make sure his heart's as big as his wallet.

SHELLEY. Yeh. Ta.

Exit SHELLEY. JAN *wakes up and reaches for her hat.*

JAN. Pearl? I'm gonna be sick.

PEARL. Not in your hat!

Scene Three

Enclosure. Minutes later. Enter SHELLEY. *She lights a cigarette and takes out the purse* LINDA *found. She hesitates, opens it and takes out the cash.*

Enter JIM McCORMACK. SHELLEY *puts the cash back in the purse and returns it to her bag.*

JIM. Have you got me? Fine. (*To camera.*) And in the fifth race of the day, the Hampton Court Stakes, Aluminum Shine has halved his odds at five to one from ten to one, and Friend of Penelope goes from eleven to four to battle two to one. It seems they don't want to know about Reno or Bust, out to seven to two from top of the head nine to four but there's good support on the exchanges for Dog Blanket, six to one. Back after the break.

JIM *puts his hand to his earpiece.*

Stay put? Right.

Aah . . . Sahara.

JIM *takes a swig from a hip flask.*

SHELLEY. How come they let you drink on the job?

JIM. They don't. But I won't tell if you won't.

SHELLEY. Why's the camera right up there?

JIM. Atmosphere.

SHELLEY. Oh.

JIM. They can take in the sights. And there's certainly some sights to see today, Sahara.

SHELLEY. What? Oh, yeh.

JIM. Where's your lady-friends?

SHELLEY. Around.

JIM. They surely haven't left you on your own?

SHELLEY. I'm just stretching me legs.

JIM. Aren't you just?

SHELLEY. Has no one ever told you it's rude to stare?

JIM. I'm not staring, I'm appreciating. Just as one would with a Matisse or a Gauguin.

SHELLEY. Oh.

JIM. May I offer you a drink?

SHELLEY. Champagne?

JIM. Maybe later.

JIM *offers her the hip flask.*

SHELLEY. Are you taking the piss?

JIM. Try it.

SHELLEY (*sniffs*). Friggin' hell, what is it?

JIM. A special blend from the McCormack distillery.

SHELLEY *wipes the top and drinks.*

SHELLEY. Bloody hell fire.

JIM. Absolutely. Chin-chin.

JIM *takes another swig.*

SHELLEY. So what's it like then? Being on telly? Do you go to loads of showbiz parties?

JIM. Of course.

SHELLEY. Do you know Jordan?

JIM. Jordan who?

SHELLEY. With the knockers? I do. Course, I call her Katie, that's her real name. I met her at a personal appearance.

JIM. Lovely girl.

SHELLEY. Do you know Posh and Becks?

JIM. My dear, when you've been around as long as I have, you know everyone.

SHELLEY. Does he really shag around?

JIM. I couldn't possibly comment.

SHELLEY. Oh, go on. Is she a cow?

JIM. They're a charming couple.

SHELLEY. Who else do you know then?

JIM. As I told you . . . everyone.

SHELLEY. But who do you know really, really well?

Beat.

JIM. Freddie Starr.

SHELLEY. Who?

JIM. Freddie Starr the comic, he's a close personal friend. And Jimmy Saville of course.

SHELLEY. Never heard of him.

JIM (*as* JIMMY). Now then, now then, how's about it guys 'n' gals.

SHELLEY. I've met loads of famous people, I have. Loads of pop stars an' presenters an' that. And I've been told on more than one occasion, I've got it.

JIM. Got what?

SHELLEY. 'It', you know? The X-Factor.

JIM. Of course. I can see it.

SHELLEY. Can yer?

JIM. Clear as the sun in the desert, Sahara.

SHELLEY. So what can you see, exactly?

JIM. Well, your personality. Your attributes. Your TV potential.

SHELLEY. Honest?

JIM. I can see you as someone like . . .

SHELLEY. Trisha.

JIM. Just like Trisha.

SHELLEY. I'd be brilliant doing Trisha 'cos I'm dead
sympathetic. I'll help anyone me, I can't help myself.

JIM. I'm sure.

SHELLEY. And if you ask me, Trisha's too 'been there, done
that'. Like, if you've cut your finger, she's broke her
bleedin' arm. It's like, 'So you went mental once, Trisha?
Get over it already.' It's pathetic.

JIM. Isn't it just?

SHELLEY. Not that I'm sat at home watching her o'course,
I'm too busy furthering my career. I like Judge Judy an' all,
have you met her? She's a real judge, you know? Are you a
real bookie?

JIM. My dear, I'm not a bookie at all. But what I could be is
your magic carpet, your Merlin, if you like.

SHELLEY. My what?

JIM. Your manager. If you so desire.

SHELLEY. You?

JIM. Why not? I know the business, the movers and shakers –
and I know television gold when I see it.

SHELLEY. Me?

JIM. Sahara, you're a natural. I've witnessed you on camera
today. You've got everything that Trisha's got and more.

JIM *hands her the microphone.*

Go on.

SHELLEY. What?

JIM. Give us your best, Trisha.

SHELLEY (*clears her throat*). 'And on today's show: Is Your
Bloke Banging Someone Else's Bird?'

JIM. Bravo!

SHELLEY. 'Girlfriend, Get Your Shit Sorted Out.'

JIM. Language.

> SHELLEY *starts to sing the chorus of 'Let Me Entertain You' by Robbie Williams.*

> I see a future here, my dear. I see a Sahara-shaped hole in the schedule.

SHELLEY. Schedule . . . ? That's a proper television word, in't it?

JIM. Schedule . . . Script . . . Shoot . . . Star. Because that's what you are, dear. That's what you are.

> *Beat.*

SHELLEY. Am I being discovered 'ere?

JIM. Discovered? You're being launched into orbit! I see paparazzi pictures – *Heat* magazine – *TV Quick* awards.

SHELLEY. No!

JIM. Celebrity Big Brother!

SHELLEY. Oh my God!

JIM. We'll make a plan over dinner tonight.

SHELLEY *(tearfully)*. I can't believe it. I can't . . .

JIM. My dear, what's the matter?

SHELLEY. Nowt. It's just me, that's all. I always get like this when summat good happens.

JIM. Come on, come here.

> *As* JIM *gives her a hug, his hands start to wander.*

SHELLEY. I've been waiting all my life for this. I want it so much. I need it.

JIM. Jim'll fix it.

SHELLEY. What are you doing?

JIM. Just retrieving my hip flask. Have another drink, that's it.

> SHELLEY *takes another gulp.*

SHELLEY. So how long will it take for me to make it?

JIM. We'll discuss it over dinner.

SHELLEY. But how long 'til my first pay-day?

JIM. Later, my dear.

SHELLEY. Do you think you'll be able to give us owt up front?

JIM. I'm sure I can.

SHELLEY. I'll have to buy stuff, won't I? Clothes an' that. I'll have to look the part, so I was wondering, can you give us a sub?

JIM. How much?

SHELLEY. A thousand pounds, that should do it.

Beat.

JIM. I'm working for you, my dear. I don't earn a penny 'til you do.

SHELLEY. Yeh but you're already on the telly, you're loaded.

JIM. Sahara, I'm sorry. It doesn't work like that.

SHELLEY. Well, how does it work?

JIM. As I said . . . I'll tell you over dinner.

Beat.

SHELLEY. Can I tell you summat first? Can I trust you?

JIM. Of course.

SHELLEY. It's nothing much, it's just I'm in a mess with money. I owe six months rent and council tax and fifteen grand on store cards and all I do is keep spending.

JIM. On what?

SHELLEY. Just clothes and shoes and jewellery, CDs, food, booze. I'm borrowing off one card to pay up another but I can't even shift the bloody interest. Then on Sunday . . .

JIM (*with hand on earpiece*). Yes?

SHELLEY. On Sunday, there's a knock on the door and it's the bailiffs.

JIM. Okay.

SHELLEY. I hid in the bedroom but I know they'll be back, I know they will, and I've got nothing to give 'em, nothing.

JIM. Standing by.

SHELLEY. I really need a few quid to get 'em off my back and I just don't know where it's gonna come from.

JIM (*to* SHELLEY). Will you shut up, woman!

SHELLEY. Sorry.

JIM (*to camera*). And they're lining up for the fifth race of the day. Reno or Bust is going out of stall one, which could be a bit of a poisoned chalice, he's had two wins in Dubai and he's in need of another today. Let's have a look at him.

SHELLEY. You don't want to manage me, do you?

JIM. Of course I do.

SHELLEY. No, you don't. It's bullshit. I've heard it all before.

JIM. Sahara –

SHELLEY. My name's not Sahara, it's Shelley.

JIM. I don't care.

SHELLEY. You're full of it.

SHELLEY *turns to go.*

JIM. I'll give you two hundred for dinner tonight.

SHELLEY. You what?

JIM. Two hundred cash. No questions asked.

SHELLEY. For dinner?

JIM. Right.

SHELLEY. And then what?

JIM. That's up to you, Sahara. I'm paying for your company, that's all.

SHELLEY. It's Shelley.

JIM. You can be whoever you want to be.

SHELLEY. Two hundred pounds for one night's work?

JIM *gives her a card.*

JIM. That's showbiz. Call me.

Exit JIM.

JIM (*voiceover*). It's the Hampton Court Stakes and they're off. Setting the pace is Aluminum Shine from Dog Blanket, Friend of Penelope and Reno or Bust.

Enter LINDA.

LINDA. Shell?

SHELLEY. Where the friggin' hell have you been?

LINDA. Talking to someone. And I'm all right now.

SHELLEY. Well, I'm glad someone is.

LINDA. What's up?

Beat.

SHELLEY. Linda, do I look like an 'ooker?

LINDA. A what?

Beat.

SHELLEY. Never mind.

SHELLEY *puts the card in her bag.*

LINDA. Listen.

JIM (*voiceover*). And Reno or Bust is snapping at the heels of Dog Blanket. Further back is Aluminum Shine. It's Dog Blanket, Reno or Bust and Aluminum Shine as they reach the final furlong, Dog Blanket leads from Reno or Bust but what a ride, he's driving hard, now it's Reno or Bust coming up on the inside, Reno or Bust inching past and Reno or Bust takes first place.

LINDA. That's us. Reno or Bust.

SHELLEY. Which race is that one?

LINDA. The fifth.

Beat.

SHELLEY. We've got five?

LINDA. Yeh.

SHELLEY. How many more do we need?

LINDA. One.

SHELLEY. Friggin' hell, Lin. Where's the girls?

Scene Four

Racetrack. Thirty minutes later. PEARL, LINDA, SHELLEY *and* JAN *stand at the front of the crowd.*

JIM (*voiceover*). And they're lining up for the last race of the day, the Buckingham Palace Stakes.

SHELLEY. Five.

PEARL. Don't get excited.

SHELLEY. Five out of six, though.

PEARL. It don't mean nothing.

SHELLEY. It means we're one-off half a million.

PEARL. Or one-off bugger all.

JIM (*voiceover*). This new race was introduced as part of the Golden Jubilee celebrations in 2002, when the meeting was first extended to five days.

JAN. Bugger-what?

PEARL. It's all right, Jan.

SHELLEY. We've nearly won the Jackpot, that's all.

JAN. Oh. Right.

SHELLEY. Which way are they running?

PEARL. The finish post's down there, look.

SHELLEY. And do we get owt for second?

PEARL. No.

SHELLEY. It's first or nothing?

PEARL. That's right.

JIM (*voiceover*). Staged on the straight course over seven
    furlongs, the final race of the day is a tricky and competitive
    handicap for three-year-olds and upward.

SHELLEY. What's the name of the horse, again?

PEARL. Broken Dreams.

LINDA. After Street of –

SHELLEY. Yeh, we know.

PEARL. It's a rank outsider.

SHELLEY. Is that good?

PEARL. Not really, no.

SHELLEY. It's gonna do it, I know it is.

LINDA. Me too. Patrick's on it.

PEARL. Patrick who?

LINDA. Patrick my friend. He's riding Broken Dreams.

SHELLEY. Since when have you known a jockey?

LINDA. Since this afternoon.

   She smiles.

PEARL. What's that smile for?

SHELLEY. What have you been up to?

LINDA. Just talking.

SHELLEY. He's took her for a roll in the hay.

LINDA. No, he never.

PEARL. Have you seen her, Jan?

JAN. I've seen two of her for the last hour.

LINDA. He's coming to Beverley on Wednesday. He's coming round for a pizza.

SHELLEY. A pizza? Well, you know what that means.

LINDA. What?

PEARL. It means they're having a pizza, that's all.

LINDA. He says he wants a Quattro Staggionni.

SHELLEY. I bet he does.

LINDA. With extra cheese.

SHELLEY. You'll be on champagne and caviar come tomorrow.

LINDA. Will I?

SHELLEY. With a shed load of designer clothes.

LINDA. I don't want designer clothes.

SHELLEY. Well, I do. I'm going straight to Harvey Nicks and then I'm getting on a plane to somewhere hot, hot, hot.

LINDA. I want to go to Whitby, my nan took me there.

JAN. I want to go to bed.

PEARL. I want to see the Aurola Borealis.

SHELLEY. The what?

PEARL. The Northern Lights.

SHELLEY. Where are they, then?

PEARL. They say Finland's a good place to see 'em.

SHELLEY. Finland? I thought you meant Scarborough or summat.

PEARL. Me and Barry watched a programme. You've never seen owt like it. They're yellow-green and blue and red, they're twisting and turning and shimmering in the sky. We said to each other we'd break the rules and go.

LINDA. Who's Barry?

Enter KEVIN, *once smartly-dressed, now dishevelled and drunk.*

SHELLEY. Never you mind.

PEARL. He's just a bloke I used to know.

LINDA. What kind of bloke?

JAN. The kind that's hard to forget.

PEARL. Well, I'm just gonna have to. It's over and done.

KEVIN. Morning, girls.

SHELLEY. Check your watch mate, it's teatime.

KEVIN *looks for his watch but he's not wearing one.*

KEVIN. Ah . . . I'm sure I had it last night.

KEVIN *sways into* PEARL, *then* SHELLEY.

PEARL. Watch it!

KEVIN. Sorry, luv. Sorry.

SHELLEY. Shift it. We wanna watch the race.

KEVIN. Having a good time, are you?

SHELLEY. We were.

KEVIN. Having fun?

PEARL. A laugh a minute.

LINDA. We've nearly won half a million.

SHELLEY. Linda!

KEVIN. Haven't we all?

SHELLEY. You can't go telling every Tom, Dick and Harry you've got money. You'll be preyed on by charlatans, you won't know who to trust.

KEVIN *looks at* JAN.

KEVIN. Does this one not say owt?

JAN. I've been unwell.

KEVIN. Oh. Okay. I'll leave you in peace. Look, I'm going. I'm gone.

SHELLEY. Good.

KEVIN. Miss?

SHELLEY. Now what?

KEVIN. Have you got a light?

SHELLEY *lights her lighter.*

SHELLEY. There.

KEVIN *stares at the flame.*

KEVIN. Have you got a cigarette?

SHELLEY. Piss off.

LINDA. It's just a cigarette, Shell.

PEARL. Go on, he might leave us alone.

SHELLEY *gives him a Sobranie Cocktail cigarette.*

SHELLEY. See yer.

KEVIN. Pink?

SHELLEY. Beggars can't be choosers.

KEVIN. No, no. (*Looks at the cigarette.*) Pink.

SHELLEY. Right first time.

SHELLEY *lights his cigarette.*

Now do one.

JAN. Are they running or what?

SHELLEY. I can't watch.

JAN. I can't focus.

LINDA. Patrick's got stars on his top.

JAN. I've got 'em in my eyes.

SHELLEY. 'And tonight, Matthew, I'm going to be loaded!'

KEVIN. Ladies?

SHELLEY. Friggin hell!

KEVIN. Can you spare a bit of change?

SHELLEY. No, and we don't want the *Big Issue* neither.

KEVIN. You see, I've lost the lads I came with . . . lost my
train ticket home . . . lost my shirt.

LINDA. You've got it on.

PEARL. He means he's broke.

KEVIN. I won on Monday, Tuesday . . .

PEARL. What? You've been here all this time?

KEVIN. I put the lot on Bearded Lady in the Gold Cup today.
Dead cert. But the jockey came off.

SHELLEY. Well, you win some, you lose some.

KEVIN. But the thing is, I've lost everything. (*Laughs.*)
Everything.

LINDA. What do you mean?

KEVIN. My wife . . . Suzanne . . . she thinks I'm on a business
trip . . . she doesn't know I lost my job . . . or why . . . or
what shit I'm in . . .

PEARL. With the horses?

KEVIN. The horses, the dogs, the fruit machines, the lot. I'd
bet on an egg and spoon race if I could. At night, I'm up on
the computer. She thinks I'm working.

JAN. And what are you doing?

KEVIN. Playing internet poker on her credit card. I'm into it
for thousands, I can't get myself out.

PEARL. Well, you've just got to get a grip, you've got to stop.

KEVIN. I've tried . . . loads of times . . . I can't.

PEARL. Yes, you can. You've got to sober up, take a big deep
breath and tell your wife.

KEVIN. But I've not even got the cash to get home . . .

SHELLEY. Friggin hell fire!

SHELLEY takes cash from her purse and gives it to KEVIN.

Is that enough?

PEARL. Bloody hell, the ice-queen melts.

SHELLEY. She can afford to.

KEVIN. I can't . . .

SHELLEY. There's no such word, mate. Just take it, ey?

PEARL takes £10 from her purse and gives it to KEVIN.

PEARL. Have a cup of tea on the train.

JAN takes food from the cool bag and gives it to KEVIN.

JAN. And a boiled egg – and a sandwich.

LINDA. And here's summat for luck.

LINDA takes off her Tony Christie badge and pins it on KEVIN.

KEVIN. Thank you, ladies. Thank you.

KEVIN kisses SHELLEY.

SHELLEY. Yeh, yeh, whatever.

KEVIN. You know, I never believed in angels 'til now.

SHELLEY. We're no angels. We're just on a winning streak.

KEVIN. But remember so was I, luv. So was I.

Exit KEVIN.

LINDA. Do you think he'll tell her?

JAN. I hope so.

PEARL. He'll have to. It catches up with them all in the end.

SHELLEY. Never mind him – they're off!

JIM (*voiceover*). And taking an early lead in the Buckingham Palace Stakes is the firm favourite Threadbare Carpet, chased by Picnic Hamper and Broken Dreams.

Sound of horses hooves and cheering crowds.

LINDA. Come on, Broken Dreams!

SHELLEY. Come on!

JIM (*voiceover*). Threadbare Carpet chased by Picnic Hamper, Broken Dreams and No Smoke Without Fire. Threadbare Carpet the clear leader, followed now on the inside by Broken Dreams. Oh, that's a bad mistake for No Smoke Without Fire, he's right out of the running now. Threadbare Carpet head to head with Broken Dreams –

LINDA. Go, Patrick!

SHELLEY. Go on!!

As the race builds to the finish, their movement becomes slow motion.

JIM (*voiceover*). Threadbare Carpet from Broken Dreams, they couldn't be closer as they head towards the line. Chasing hard is Picnic Hamper but he's still got a few lengths to find. Into the final furlong, it's Threadbare Carpet and Broken Dreams, looks like a photo finish, what battlers these horses are, Threadbare Carpet now inching away, it's Threadbare Carpet from Broken Dreams, still Threadbare Carpet, and he's there! Threadbare Carpet first, Broken Dreams second. Picnic Hamper third.

Silence.

SHELLEY. Second.

PEARL. That's that, then.

JAN. Does that mean we can go?

LINDA. He did his best.

SHELLEY. We've lost. We've friggin' lost.

SHELLEY screws the betting slip up and throws it on the floor.

LINDA. It weren't Patrick's fault.

PEARL. We know.

LINDA. D'you think he heard us shouting?

JAN. Course.

LINDA. He did his best.

PEARL. Come on. It's time we weren't here.

SHELLEY *takes out* JIM's *card.*

LINDA. Shelley?

SHELLEY. It's all right. You get off. I'm staying.

PEARL. What are you on about?

SHELLEY. You're not the only one to find a bloke, Lin. I've met one an' all. He's goodlooking and he's loaded. He works in the media and he wants to wine and dine me.

PEARL. Where?

SHELLEY. At his posh hotel. So that's what I'm doing. See yer.

PEARL. What's going on, Shell?

SHELLEY. Nowt.

PEARL. You can't kid a kidder. What?

SHELLEY. It's true. I've clicked.

PEARL. If you had, you'd not have shut up about it. I don't know what you're up to but you're coming back with us.

SHELLEY. Please, Pearl. I can't.

PEARL. Can't what?

SHELLEY. I can't go back there. The factory, the flat, I can't face it any more.

JAN. What's she on about?

SHELLEY. If I go back now, I'll never get out. I'll never have none of the stuff we've seen today. I'll never be famous. I can't sing or dance or act or owt, there's nothing I can do except for . . .

JAN. What?

SHELLEY. I've got nothing to go back for, I've got no one to go out with. I've got nothing. I've got less than nothing.

PEARL. You've got us.

JAN. You have, Shell.

LINDA. Come out with me and Patrick next week.

SHELLEY *(faltering)*. Don't. Don't be nice to me, I can't stand it.

LINDA. Shelley . . .

PEARL. All right. Have it your way. Get your arse on that bleedin' bus now.

SHELLEY. But –

PEARL. Now!

SHELLEY *takes the purse from her bag.*

SHELLEY. Shall we hand this in first? It's the right thing to do, in't it?

JAN. Come on, then.

LINDA *(puts out her hand to* SHELLEY*)*. Let's go.

Exit SHELLEY, *with* JAN *and* LINDA. PEARL *takes a last look around, then goes to follow them. Enter* BARRY, *a bookie. He picks up the betting slip.*

BARRY. Pearl.

PEARL *turns.*

PEARL. Barry?

BARRY. How are you?

PEARL. I thought you weren't . . .

BARRY. What?

PEARL. I didn't see you there, that's all.

BARRY. I know. So what are you doing here?

PEARL. It's Ladies' Day. I'm out with the girls.

BARRY. Quite a spectacle, in't it?

PEARL. You can say that again.

BARRY. I like your hat.

PEARL. Ta.

BARRY. I've seen it before.

PEARL. Have you?

BARRY. The Station Hotel. You wore it that first time.

PEARL. Perhaps I did, I don't recall.

BARRY. You're looking good, luv.

PEARL. Ta.

BARRY. How's the family?

PEARL. Fine.

BARRY. Work?

PEARL. The same.

BARRY. And you?

Beat.

PEARL. The girls . . . they'll be waiting.

BARRY. They're all right for a minute. Tell me, really, how you are.

PEARL. Just glad to see you. Come here.

PEARL *goes to kiss* BARRY *but he steps back.*

BARRY. No.

PEARL. No one's gonna see us.

BARRY. I know.

PEARL. So what's the matter?

BARRY. Pearl, we need to talk.

PEARL. It's all right. I get it.

BARRY. What?

PEARL. You've come here with your wife.

BARRY. No.

PEARL. Does she know about you and me. Is that why you –

BARRY. No.

PEARL. Have you met someone else, then?

BARRY. No.

PEARL. Did you just get bored of me, is that it?

BARRY. No way.

PEARL. So what happened? I waited all night in that hotel bar for you. I had visions of your car in a ditch. I rang the hospital and everything.

BARRY. I weren't there.

PEARL. I know that much. So where were you?

BARRY *looks at the betting slip.*

BARRY. Broken Dreams.

PEARL. Where?

BARRY *hands the slip to* PEARL.

BARRY. Take it.

PEARL. It's no good to us now.

BARRY. Just have it as a souvenir or summat.

PEARL. Can we forget about the horses and talk about us?

BARRY. Fine. What bit of us do you want to talk about?

PEARL. What do you think?

BARRY. The time we watched Wimbledon with champagne and strawberries? Or the day we overslept and you had to phone in sick and we didn't leave the hotel 'til the maids chucked us out.

PEARL. So they did.

BARRY. Or that night when you told me you'd leave Mick if I'd leave Anne. Remember that?

PEARL. I remember you said no.

BARRY. Why? What did I tell you?

PEARL. Oh, the kids, the house, the money. All the reasons I couldn't do it either in the cold light of day.

BARRY. I was lying. I was covering up. I couldn't leave 'cos I was frightened.

PEARL. Of what?

BARRY. Of you. Of us. Of what I was feeling. So long as I could keep it locked in that room, I was all right. The thought of opening the door on it all . . .

PEARL. What?

BARRY. When you're a kid, you're afraid of the dark but you grow up and grow out of it, don't you? In time, you think you're strong, you think that nothing can touch you. Then one day you find it's not the darkness that scares you, it's the light.

PEARL. What do you mean?

BARRY. I was hiding in that hotel room. Not from my wife or the world. From myself.

PEARL. Barry –

BARRY. I should have opened up and let you in, I know that now. I should have told you exactly how I felt.

PEARL. You did.

BARRY. I mean, what was I thinking of? What was I on? I should have had the guts to say I loved you.

PEARL. But that weren't in the rules.

BARRY. Nor was coming here today but you did.

PEARL. I wanted to see you.

BARRY. Why?

PEARL. To find out what went wrong.

BARRY. Why?

PEARL. 'Cos I needed to know.

BARRY. Yes, I know but tell me why?

PEARL. Why d'you think? 'Cos I love you too.

Beat.

BARRY. We should never have played by the rules, Pearl.

PEARL. Well, we did.

BARRY. Thanks to them, no one knew to let you know.

PEARL. Know what?

BARRY. I was at home that Thursday night. Packing my stuff to come to see you. I was reaching up to the top of the wardrobe for my suitcase. Felt a pain all down my left arm, then it spread to my chest.

PEARL. No.

BARRY. I don't remember nothing more after that.

PEARL. Barry . . .

BARRY. It's all right.

PEARL. But if I'd known, I'd have never . . . I'd have found some way to see you. If you'd left word at the hotel, I'd have come.

BARRY. I know you would.

PEARL. I mean, stuff the rules, you could have . . .

PEARL *is touching his face.*

BARRY. What?

PEARL. You're cold.

BARRY. I know.

PEARL. It's summer.

BARRY. And you know what? You look lovely in the sunlight.

PEARL. Am I dreaming this?

BARRY. No.

PEARL. Am I?

BARRY. It was real, you and me. That's what I've come to tell you. It was real.

PEARL. You're not coming back, are you?

BARRY. No. Not this time.

PEARL. I knew it. Deep down, I knew you wouldn't go without saying goodbye.

BARRY. You wouldn't let me.

PEARL. But now I've got to.

BARRY. Now you've got to go to all them places I can't. Now you've got to live it for the both of us.

Beat.

PEARL. So what now?

BARRY. Last dance.

PEARL. Here? It's a racecourse.

BARRY. And rules are for breaking.

Music. Lights. They dance.

Scene Five

Fish plant. Next morning. Enter SHELLEY, LINDA *and* JAN. *They gloomily set up for the working day.*

SHELLEY. Lin?

LINDA. What?

SHELLEY. Where's the sharpener?

LINDA *passes* SHELLEY *the knife sharpener.* SHELLEY *sharpens her knife angrily.*

LINDA. Steady on, Shell.

JAN. You're trimming, not committing hari-kari.

SHELLEY. Don't bet on it.

Beat.

LINDA. Where's Pearl?

JAN. Sorting out her papers in the office.

LINDA. Do you think she'll change her mind?

JAN. No.

LINDA. But Maud retired and came back a month later.

SHELLEY. More fool her.

LINDA. She missed us.

JAN. Pearl won't.

LINDA. She's got Mick, I suppose.

SHELLEY. She's got Patrington Haven.

JAN. We'll have to have a day trip, would you like that?

LINDA. Oh yeh.

SHELLEY. Well, that's summat to live for, in't it?

The machines strike up. They start trimming and packing.

JAN. What did you have for your tea when you got home?

LINDA. Pizza.

SHELLEY. Cyanide.

JAN. Come on, Shell. It weren't that bad.

SHELLEY. What a friggin' waste of a day.

LINDA. Not for me.

SHELLEY. Yeh, all right, bighead.

JAN. It's all a bit of a blur.

SHELLEY. Well, let me remind you. There was no Posh, no
    Becks, not even Tony friggin' Christie.

LINDA. It dun't matter.

SHELLEY. Oh, so now you've got Patrick, Tony Christie's old news?

LINDA. I've not got him. He's just coming round.

SHELLEY. For a little bit of sha-la-la-la-la-la-la-la.

JAN (*winces*). Shell!

SHELLEY. Hair of the dog, that's what you need.

JAN. No chance. I'm never gonna drink again.

SHELLEY. Double vodka, that'd do it.

JAN. Our Claire had her exam yesterday.

LINDA. Did she pass?

JAN. We won't know 'til August but she's confident. She got the George Eliot question.

SHELLEY. Never mind him –

JAN. Her.

SHELLEY. What did she say when she saw the state of you?

JAN. Well, as a matter of fact, she said, 'Mum, you should do this more often.'

SHELLEY. Yeh? Nice one, Claire.

JAN. She says if I've gorra life, it'll help her to go.

SHELLEY. And you don't have to go far to get one.

JAN. What do you mean?

LINDA. I couldn't sleep last night.

JAN. Shell?

SHELLEY. Nor me. I kept thinking what I woulda done with all that cash.

JAN. I'd put Claire through University. Buy her a car.

SHELLEY. I'd pay off my store cards. Move to a flat on the Marina. Jack my job in and start my own salon.

LINDA. You'd be dead good at that.

SHELLEY. I know I would. I'd do hair and beauty, women and men. I'd get all the City lads in. I'd call it Shelley's.

JAN. Would you do us a discount?

SHELLEY. Would I 'ell. You could come in on a Monday when it's quiet.

JAN. What would you have done with the money, Lin?

SHELLEY. Given the lot to her mum.

LINDA. I wouldn't. She's gone.

SHELLEY. What do you mean gone?

LINDA. I went home last night and told her 'Go' – and she did.

JAN. Really?

LINDA. Some things are scary but you've still gotta do 'em, an't yer?

SHELLEY. So this wouldn't have owt to do with Patrick coming up?

LINDA. It might.

SHELLEY. Get you!

JAN. You really like him, don't you?

LINDA. He just talks to me nice. Like I matter, you know?

SHELLEY. We'll go to town on Sat'day, get you summat to wear.

JAN. Nowt tarty though.

SHELLEY. You can come an' all, Jan. It's time you dressed to impress. We'll get your hair done.

JAN. What's wrong with my hair?

SHELLEY. Nowt that a bottle of bleach won't fix.

JAN. I'm all right the way I am.

SHELLEY. You've got to look your best for J – O – E.

LINDA. You what?

SHELLEY. Joe.

JAN. What about him?

SHELLEY. You know what, you snogged him.

LINDA. Yesterday?

SHELLEY. At that wedding; and you've fancied the pants of him since.

LINDA. Have you, Jan?

JAN. How do you know that?

SHELLEY. You told me. Well, you told the whole of Royal Ascot.

JAN. No!?

SHELLEY. Oh yes. And if you don't do summat about it, I will.

JAN. There's no point now, is there? He's going away.

SHELLEY. But he might take you with him.

JAN. Don't be ridiculous. I couldn't afford that, not with Claire –

Enter PEARL.

PEARL. Never say never, luv. You'd be great together.

JAN. I told you an' all?

PEARL. You didn't have to. It's been obvious for years.

JAN. Has it?

PEARL. I weren't the only one with a secret, was I?

PEARL *starts working.*

JAN. Pearl, I think I owe you an apology.

PEARL. No, you don't.

JAN. Yes, I do, I said some things I –

PEARL. Forget 'em.

JAN. We won't let it come between us, will we? I mean, I'm not gonna lose you 'cos of a bloke?

PEARL. No way.

JAN. I'm sorry he weren't there for you. I know what it meant.

PEARL. Yeh.

JAN. But perhaps it's for the best, ey? Perhaps it means you can get on with your life?

PEARL. You're right. You've got to find a way to lay these things to rest. Be glad it happened and say your goodbyes.

Enter JOE.

JOE. Morning, girls.

SHELLEY. Morning, Joe.

PEARL. Morning.

JAN. Yeh, morning.

JOE. Well, you owe me a beer or three.

PEARL. You covered us all right?

JOE. Oh aye. We got twice the output from the agency lasses.

SHELLEY. Yeh, right.

PEARL. Ta, Joe.

JAN. Yeh. Ta.

JOE. So how was it?

SHELLEY. Don't ask.

JOE. Well, I am.

LINDA. It were brilliant.

PEARL. We met that Jim McCormack.

LINDA. We nearly won the jackpot.

SHELLEY (*gesturing to* JAN). And someone got shit-faced.

JOE. I didn't know you liked a drink?

SHELLEY. Well, there's a lot of things about Jan you don't know.

JAN (*quickly*). Linda met a fella.

SHELLEY. He's a jockey.

JOE. Oh aye?

LINDA. He's coming for a pizza next Wednesday.

SHELLEY. Perhaps Joe might like to come?

LINDA. Ey?

JOE. You're all right.

SHELLEY. She's having a party, aren't you, Lin? I'm gonna be there . . . and Pearl . . . and Jan.

JAN. Am I?

SHELLEY. It's gonna be a right laugh, ey Lin?

LINDA. Er . . . yeh.

SHELLEY. We'll get you them beers in, how about it?

JOE. I think I'll give it a miss. I've got stuff to do next week.

JAN. Me too.

JOE. Going away stuff, you know?

JAN. Claire stuff.

JOE. Sorry an' all that.

JAN. Sorry.

Beat.

JOE. Right. I'd best get on.

JAN. Me an' all.

SHELLEY. Jan?!

Beat.

JAN. Joe?

JOE. Yeh?

Beat.

JAN. I've changed my mind. I'm going.

JOE. Oh?

JAN. And I'd like you to come . . . if you've got time before you go?

JOE. Would you?

JAN. Yeh. If you want to?

Beat.

JOE. He's a jockey, this fella?

JAN. Yeh.

JOE. I've never met a jockey.

JAN. Well, you'd find it very interesting.

JOE. I could ask him what went off in that last race. Was he in it?

LINDA. He was riding Broken Dreams.

JOE. Broken Dreams? He never was.

LINDA. He came second.

JOE. No, he didn't.

LINDA. He did.

JOE. There was a right argy-bargy, did you not see it?

SHELLEY. No.

JAN. What happened?

JOE. There was a steward's enquiry, it's all over the papers. The winner was disqualified for careless riding. Broken Dreams came first.

PEARL. No?

JOE. I read it in the *Mirror* this morning. And the best of it is, some Jackpot punter –

PEARL. Oh my God.

JAN. Oh my God.

SHELLEY. That's us! That's us! We had five – now we've got six.

JAN. Six?

LINDA. That's the lot.

JOE. Let's have a look at the slip, then?

SHELLEY. The what?

JOE. The betting slip.

SHELLEY. I've not got it.

LINDA. Shelley screwed it up and threw it away.

JAN. But there must be some record on computer or summat?

JOE. If you've not got the slip, you've had it.

JAN. Tell us you've got it, Shelley? Tell us.

SHELLEY. No. No!

PEARL. No.

PEARL *takes a betting slip out of her pocket.*

I have.

JOE *takes the betting slip.*

JOE. Tony's Lad; Solitaire; Blind Alley; Sweet Maria; Reno or Bust; Broken Dreams. No?

PEARL/SHELLEY/LINDA/JAN. Yes!!

The End.